Colossians

Set Your Heart on Things Above

A Bible Study by Tracy Hill

ISBN: 978-0-9976913-7-5

Dedicated to...

Grandma Mary, the one who taught me to make chocolate chip cookies and showed me how to search the heavens and count the stars.

I can't wait to see you in Heaven someday!

Contents

Foreword

The Holy Bible is the most life-changing, impactful resource we have access to. It is the very Word of God, given to us by God Himself. It is a revelation of who He is in all His glorious majesty; it is a disclosing of His plan for mankind since the beginning of time on into eternity; it is a declaration of His purpose for every individual human being. The Bible is the most powerful book ever written and it has endured throughout the centuries, reaching to the ends of the earth. The Word of God has the power to redeem, renew, revive, and restore what is broken. It speaks life, truth, love, grace, mercy, hope, healing, peace, and joy to those who read it earnestly desiring to hear from God. It is inspired by our Heavenly Father, and it is His Message revealed to the world and to each of us personally—His Message points us to Jesus, our Savior.

As we mine the pearls of wisdom found in the book of Colossians, I pray that you are blessed and inspired by what God personally speaks to you. I pray that you come to a deeper understanding of who Jesus is and what that means for your day-to-day life. I pray for the Holy Spirit to infuse the words to be more than writings on a page, that they would come alive and impact your life in new and miraculous ways. Before you open your Bible and begin your study time, I encourage you to pause and pray these things for yourself also.

What a great blessing we have in holding such a magnificent treasure in our hands, having God's guidance, comfort, and promises at our very fingertips! I cannot wait to delve into the Scriptures with you and discover the spiritual riches of unfathomable worth that God has in store for us! Let's begin!

"My goal is that they may be encouraged in heart and united in love, so that they may have the full riches of complete understanding, in order that they may know the mystery of God, namely, Christ, in whom are hidden all the treasures of wisdom and knowledge." Colossians 2:2-3

The Cover Photo

When I began writing this study and God placed the title of the book on my heart, I knew immediately the picture I wanted on the front cover. My home is nestled at the foot of the Santa Monica Mountain range. There is a mountain out my front door, and hills are all around. I walk about my neighborhood surrounded by their grandeur almost daily—usually in solitude with the Lord. The photo on the cover of this book is of a California state park located practically in my backyard. I hike there with my sons and my dear neighbor and friend. The beauty changes throughout the year— Spring is when the fields are green, and the flowers are in full bloom; the Fall casts a warm golden hue over everything. I usually skip the trails and stick to the streets during the summer months, because that's when the snakes come out. No matter what time of year it happens to be, these mountains remind me of a very poignant verse, Psalm 121.

"I lift up my eyes to the mountains— where does my help come from? My help comes from the LORD, the Maker of heaven and earth." Psalm 121:1-2

The words of this Psalm have even been written into a song, and on occasion I sing the tune aloud to myself. Whether I'm having a great day or facing some difficulties, these promises of God bring comfort to my heart and joy to my mind. I purposefully lift my eyes and remember that my help comes from God who formed these towering mountains with greater ease than we make sandcastles at the beach. He is Lord over all, Creator of the heavens and earth. He is more than capable of taking care of my life, and yours. He is our help in the day of trouble and our source of peace despite circumstances. He is our hope for today and tomorrow; He is our strength for whatever comes our way. God alone is our steadfast provider, sustainer, and protector.

Let's lift our eyes to the mountains and remember that God is on the throne!

Introduction

The book of *Colossians* is just as relevant to our Christian faith today as it was to the early church when written nearly two thousand years ago. Colossians is full of affirmation as to the identity of Jesus Christ, reminding us that our salvation is complete in Him alone. Throughout this study we will encounter passionate exhortations to keep our eyes focused on the Lord, always mindful of our identity in Christ. We will find authoritative teachings that remind us of God's truth, better enabling us to recognize the lies and deception of the world. We will delve into a wide array of lessons which equip us for our daily life in Christ.

Colossians is a letter written by a man named Paul sometime between the years 60-62 AD, to a real church in the city of Colossae. Paul was a God-appointed apostle of Jesus Christ. If you are not yet familiar with him, rest assured, you will be very soon. Paul was a man on fire for the Lord, an unstoppable force empowered by the Holy Spirit, set on spreading the Gospel to the ends of the earth. Paul wrote many letters to various churches and individuals as a means of encouraging their faith and keeping them on course with true Biblical teachings.

Paul wrote this letter as he sat confined as a prisoner in Rome. He never let his circumstances obscure the hope he personally had in Jesus or hinder the hope he resolutely wanted to share. Even chains could not restrain Paul's ministry to the church or squelch his faith in Jesus. He proclaimed the Gospel until his dying breath. He encouraged and preached to those who came to visit him in prison as the guards who stood watch over him listened in; and to the churches he had planted, and the churches he had not had chance to visit. While Paul did not personally establish the Colossian church, he did plant the church at Ephesus during his three-year ministry there. The cities of Ephesus and Colossae were approximately one hundred miles apart, and by the joyful word of mouth, the Gospel had spread to this and many other cities. Evidently a man named Epaphras had a hand in founding the church of Colossae. He heard the Good News of the Gospel while visiting Ephesus, gave his life to Christ, and upon his return home started the church at Colossae. The church was comprised of a predominantly Gentile population who had no previous relationship with the God of the Bible. (A Gentile is anyone who is not Jewish.)

In the 5th century B.C. Colossae had been a prosperous city located along a major trade route in the Roman territory of Asia Minor, now known as modern day Turkey. By Paul's time, trade routes had been moved and the city had declined. Even though the city's prosperity waned, many of the pagan philosophies from Greeks, Romans, and the Far East remained. Colossae was inundated with ideologies and religions of travelers who passed through and those who settled in to live. Legalistic views also prevailed among the population due to a large Jewish settlement of those who fled terrible persecution from Antioch Epiphanes in 223-187 B.C.

The Colossian church started off strong but as we'll glean from Paul's letter to them, some Christians had begun to fall back into old patterns or absorb and incorporate various ideas from the surrounding culture into their beliefs. They combined teachings from Judaism, paganism, and Greek thought with their Christian faith, eventually resulting in heresies known as Gnosticism, asceticism and mysticism (we will cover that more in our lessons). The letter to the Colossian congregants was intended to correct and combat false teachings that had infiltrated the church and encourage believers to stand firm on the rock-solid truth of Jesus alone. Paul reaffirmed Jesus' deity and reminded them that His sacrifice on the Cross is all-sufficient in reconciling them to God. He reminded the reader that in Jesus there is fullness of life and an abundance of every good thing. The letter went on to detail the godly characteristics their new lives should overflow with because of their salvation and forgiveness from God.

We will study this letter with the purpose of taking the words to heart for ourselves. Paul's letter focuses on who Christ is, what Christ has done for us, who we are in Christ, and how as believers we should live in response. The letter to the Colossians is ultimately a message for all Christians to stand firm in their faith in Jesus and grow accordingly. It is a call to lean into the Lord more closely and press on, confident in our God-given identity.

Paul addresses a variety of topics reminding us of how our Christian faith should impact our day-to-day lives. He touches on subjects such as: the sufficiency of Christ in all things, our identity in Christ, our prayer life, our home life, our character, our speech, our ministry, and our relationships with one another.

Paul's letter instructs us in Biblical truth, showing us God's will and purpose for our lives. Looking to the Lord, believing His Words, and living according to His plan always leads to abundant blessings.

"So be careful to do what the LORD *your God has commanded you; do not turn aside to the right or to the left.* [33] *Walk in obedience to all that the* LORD *your God has commanded you, so that you may live and prosper and prolong your days in the land that you will possess." Deuteronomy 5:32-33*

Throughout this study we will redirect our minds onto God's Word—not on the news, social media, popular opinion, or even our friends' advice. We are going to fill our minds with words that are full of promise and Biblical teachings that have endured throughout the generations. By founding our lives on what God says, we'll find that we are less likely to be shaken by the things going on around us.

Even though we're studying the book of Colossians, we'll also be looking up verses throughout the entire Bible. (I love seeing how all of Scripture ties together!) The *Table of Contents* can be a great resource in helping you navigate your way through God's Word.

I have recorded short summary videos to accompany and enhance your study. Watch the *Introduction* video *before* you begin the study. Please enjoy all the others *after* you have completed each lesson.

You can find them on my website:

https://www.beblessedandinspired.com/videos

You can also listen in a podcast format if you like.

On Spotify: Be Blessed and Inspired with Tracy Hill

"Since then, you have been raised with Christ, set your hearts on

things above, where Christ is, seated at the right hand of

God. Set your minds on things above, not on earthly things."

Colossians 3:1-2

Hope in Christ

Colossians 1:1-14

When was the last time you received a letter in the mail? It seems that texting and emails have taken over as the more efficient means of communicating, but I still think letters are much more personal and heartwarming. Don't you agree? Fortunately for us, Colossians was composed at a time when ink and paper were all the rage. Since the book of Colossians was written as *a letter* to a group of believers, let's read it as such for ourselves. We will familiarize ourselves with its entire message and then revisit and ponder it section by section to better grasp the contents.

Please open your Bible and read the complete book of Colossians in one sitting. Don't feel overwhelmed—although it is packed with important information, it is only four chapters long. This is just to get a feel for the flow of the letter and a brief overview of the themes. I find that while Bible apps are useful for looking up specific verses, reading directly from the pages of the Bible is most effective for in-depth study of God's Word. You can hold the Book in your hands, feel the weight of the pages, meditate on the gravity of the words as you pause and linger over the sentences and phrases. I will be using the NIV version, but feel free to read and use whichever version you are most comfortable with.

1. What main themes do you observe from your initial read-through of Colossians 1:1-4:18?

2. What is the overall tone of the letter? What feelings and encouragements do you initially come away with?

3. Do you find any of the topics difficult to understand? Which ones?

4. Which portions are you looking forward to studying more in-depth?

Now that we have established our overview of the letter, let's slow it down, savor the words, and tuck the messages more securely into our hearts. For the duration of this lesson, we will focus on **Colossians 1:1-14**. Please reread these verses to lay the foundation of what we will cover.

The Authors

Colossians 1:1, *"Paul, an apostle of Christ Jesus by the will of God, and Timothy our brother,"*

We don't have to jump to the bottom of this letter to discover the author—we are told his identity right up front. Paul, the author of the letter, was not one of the original twelve disciples turned apostles. He was not even among the crowd who followed Jesus during His earthly ministry. **In Acts 9** we learn that Paul was a strict religious Jew who sought to stop the spread of the Gospel. He was present at and gave approval of the persecution and killing of Jesus' followers. He was vehemently against the church—it was on his way to arrest Christians that he personally and miraculously encountered the resurrected Jesus. Despite his past opposition, the Lord sought him out and specifically chose him to be a leader in the church. Paul immediately went from opposing Christ, to being His greatest proponent. His transformation served as an undeniable testimony to the power and grace of God. He went on numerous missionary journeys, spreading the Gospel throughout the Mediterranean region. He faced ridicule, abuse, threats, jail, and ultimately death for the sake of his faith in Jesus. His life was radically changed by his encounter with the Savior. With his eyes firmly fixed on Jesus he was able to endure many things, always maintaining a mindset of patience, peace, hope, and joy.

5. Read **Acts 9:1-31** to witness Paul's transformation for yourself. How does this prove that anyone can change by giving their life to Jesus?

6. What drastic measures did the Lord take to get Saul's attention? What question did Jesus ask Saul, and who did Jesus say He is in response?

7. What do you observe regarding God's amazing grace?

8. Describe Saul/Paul's radical repentance and new passion.

9. How did the other disciples and Christians initially respond?

Saul found his hope in the Lord and became Paul. In **Acts 9:29-30** we see the tables are turned and Paul is being pursued and his life is at risk. He has chosen to lay down his life to follow Jesus. He is a new creation in Christ.

Timothy, his co-author, was a young man whom Paul discipled and trained to be a leader in the church. They were brothers-in-Christ who left everything behind for the sake of following Jesus!

10. Turn to **Acts 16:1-5** in your Bibles and read the brief account of Timothy's initial meeting with Paul. How is Timothy's family described? Who most likely shared their faith with him? (See also **2 Timothy 1:5**)

11. What procedure did Timothy undergo for the sake of preaching the Gospel to the Jews? How does this display his dedication?

Both Paul and Timothy were *all in* for the Lord. They were ready to do anything, go anywhere, and reach anyone and everyone for the sake of Christ. They fully grasped the hope that Jesus brings to all people and were resolute on sharing it!

Throughout the New Testament we find Timothy's name included in the list of early believers who traveled the world declaring the Good News of salvation through Jesus' death, burial, and resurrection. **1 Timothy 1:2** reveals the close bond between Paul and Timothy, *"To Timothy my true son in the faith: Grace, mercy and peace from God the Father and Christ Jesus our Lord."*

In the opening words of this letter to the Colossians we read that Timothy is together with Paul in sending encouraging reminders to the church of Colossae. Their sole purpose was to make sure believers did not drift from the truth of who Jesus is, either by falling back into old patterns and beliefs, or by mixing in new philosophies with their faith. We'll read more on this message throughout the letter.

Learning about the lives of the saints in the Bible is a wonderful way to learn more about God and reflect on our own walk with the Lord. According to the New Testament we are saints too.

"Now, therefore, you are no longer strangers and foreigners, but fellow citizens with the saints and members of the household of God..." Ephesians 2:19

So, let's make this personal.

12. Reflect on your first encounter with Jesus. How and when did you first meet your Savior? Who shared Jesus with you? What did they say?

13. Think about your daily encounters with Jesus. Describe your emotions during these divine appointments—surprise, comfort, peace, joy, contentment, etc.....

14. How has your life been impacted and transformed as a direct result of your encounter with Jesus? Do people notice a difference in you because of your relationship with the Lord? Would people say you are *all in* for Jesus? Would you describe yourself as *all in* with Him?

The Recipients

Colossians 1:2a, *"To God's holy people in Colossae, the faithful brothers and sisters in Christ:"*

Paul and Timothy wrote not to the world of unbelievers, but to the church of Colossae, which is in modern-day Turkey; these were God's holy people, who had placed their faith in Jesus as Savior and were set apart and living for Him. In his greeting Paul addresses them as *faithful brothers and sisters in Christ*—essentially reminding them of their common bond of faith and shared love for Jesus. Does the church always walk in harmony and love with our fellow Christians? I'm afraid not. Do individuals like you and me always live in the reality of our amazing identity? I'm sorry to say that we don't always.

The phrase *in Christ* describes those who have confessed and repented of their sin and placed their faith in Jesus' sacrifice to make them right with God. Being *in Christ* confers us a right standing before God. It cleanses us from the stains of our past, and it gives us a brand-new, born-again lease on life. Our position *in Christ* gives us access to the supernatural power of God, which is at work in, for, and through us. Being *in Christ* grants us citizenship in the Kingdom of Heaven where we will spend eternity with our Heavenly Father. *In Christ* we are washed in the Lord's righteousness and wrapped in God's love.

15. To fully experience the abundant life that Jesus came to give us, we must remember our identity *in Christ*—we are loved, forgiven, saved, set free, blessed, embraced. And we join God's family with other believers. What aspect of your God-given identity do you need to grasp more fully? Ask the Lord to help you believe and step into the fullness of who He has made you to be *in Christ*.

    I encourage you to use this space to write short a prayer now:

From God

Colossians 1:2b, *"Grace and peace to you from God our Father."*

This short phrase contains important information and powerful reminders—the God who reigns from Heaven above, the Creator of the entire universe is also our Heavenly *Father*. And we get to approach Him as such! He is the author of absolute forgiveness and mercy, and the source of all true and lasting peace! We are meant to live in the newness of His grace every day. Abiding in Him is the best way to experience His blessings.

16. God is a different kind of father from any earthly dad. His love is absolutely pure, perfect, and unconditional. What does it mean for you to approach God as your Heavenly Father?

17. Take a moment to meditate on God's amazing grace. How does His grace impact your eternity and each new morning?

18. Describe a time when you were washed in God's unshakeable peace.

"And the peace of God, which transcends all understanding, will guard your hearts and your minds in Christ Jesus." Philippians 4:7

19. Delve into the following verses and make note of what you learn regarding the importance of focusing our thoughts on the Lord:

- **Psalm 1:1-3**

- **Psalm 19:14**

- **Psalm 48:9**

- **Psalm 77:12**

- **Romans 12:2**

- **James 1:6-8**

To meditate on the Word of God is to *muse and ponder; to deeply think upon and securely tuck in your heart* the wonderful promises and ways of the Lord. Be sure to fix your mind and heart on Jesus and meditate on the Scriptures regularly.

Springing from Hope

The following verses encompass Paul's prayer for us:

Colossians 1:3-6a, *"We always thank God, the Father of our Lord Jesus Christ, when we pray for you, ⁴ because we have heard of your faith in Christ Jesus and of the love you have for all God's people— ⁵ the faith and love that spring from the hope stored up for you in heaven and about which you have already heard in the true message of the gospel ⁶ that has come to you."*

Paul states that he and Timothy always pray for the church at Colossae, and I'm sure if he were here today, he'd be praying for us too. Paul was a man of prayer— he knew what an invaluable and powerful resource it is to bring our requests to the Lord. He also placed great value on giving thanks to the Lord, no matter our circumstances—our salvation alone gives us so much to be grateful for!

20. For what two things does Paul commend the Colossian church? Why are these so important?

Paul affirms that he has heard about their strong faith in Jesus Christ and their holy love for each other. He doesn't say he has heard about their religiosity, their staunch political stance, or their personal opinions of various matters. He is concerned with and proud of their unwavering faith in Jesus and the way they treat their brothers and sisters-in-Christ, even when they disagree.

21. Please read **John 13:34-35** and record what Jesus told His followers. How is love a more accurate and effective testimony to who Jesus is, the hope He offers, and the power He has in our lives?

22. How well do you see Jesus' love being lived out in the church today? How could we do better? Give some examples.

23. What does Paul say our faith and love should spring from? How important is it for us to keep this hope in mind?

Children of God have the hope of being with Jesus forever in Heaven. We live as citizens of His Heavenly Kingdom while dwelling here on earth. Our future hope affects our lives here and now by lifting our eyes to Jesus, focusing our minds on His Truth, strengthening us for our daily journey, and helping us to love sacrificially like our Savior!

24. How is this hope-filled expectation affecting your life? How often are you aware of this promise—always, frequently, or does it rarely come to mind? Explain.

I encourage you to bear your future hope in mind every day and let it impact your faith and love for others right now.

God's Grace

Colossians 1:6b, *"In the same way, the gospel is bearing fruit and growing throughout the whole world—just as it has been doing among you since the day you heard it and truly understood God's grace."*

The Good News of Jesus has been spreading around the globe since He stepped out of the grave. It is still changing lives to this very day! It thrives despite opposition; it flourishes despite persecution. The Gospel has been bringing light to dark places for centuries; it has been setting captives free throughout generations. God's amazing grace covers our sins and gives us new life. His wonderful grace continues impacting lives—filling us with hope, peace, and joy, giving us a new focus, perspective, and purpose.

According to Biblehub.com the Greek root meaning of *grace* as used in the verse is: *"kindness; grace as a gift or blessing brought to man by Jesus Christ; favor; gratitude; thanks."*

25. As you reflect on God's grace what emotions wash over you?

26. How can you more readily offer grace to others? Who specifically is God nudging you to show more grace to? Ask for His help in doing so.

Truly understanding God's grace towards us changes our hearts and bears fruit in our lives.

Love in the Spirit

Colossians 1:7-8, *"You learned it from Epaphras, our dear fellow servant, who is a faithful minister of Christ on our behalf, ⁸ and who also told us of your love in the Spirit."*

Paul commends his friend Epaphras as a *dear fellow servant*—pursuing the same purpose of glorifying the Lord. In the church we are all meant to work together for the sake of Jesus Christ. There should be no competition, everyone is essential in sharing the Good News. Here we also see that Paul praises the people's love for one another *in the Spirit*. Living sacrificially like Jesus cannot be done apart from the Holy Spirit's transforming work in us. On our own, insecurities, pride, and selfishness get in the way. But the Spirit works unity and love among us!

27. **1 Corinthians 13:4-8** describes God's love. Please read these verses and complete the following phrases:

   - *Love is...*

   - *It does/is not...*

   - *It always....*

   - *Love never...*

28. God's love is our flawless standard. With the Spirit's help, this is the love we are called to exhibit. Describe how the Lord's love fills you up. How can you more freely overflow with God's love to others?

The more we are filled with God's love, the more naturally and effortlessly we love like He does. Reflect on God's generous love towards you, lean into Him more, allow Him to change your heart, and ask Him to overflow through your life.

Pray Continually

Colossians 1:9-10, *"For this reason, since the day we heard about you, we have not stopped praying for you. We continually ask God to fill you with the knowledge of his will through all the wisdom and understanding that the Spirit gives, [10] so that you may live a life worthy of the Lord and please him in every way: bearing fruit in every good work, growing in the knowledge of God..."*

29. How would you describe your prayer life? How often do you pray? What kind of requests do you usually bring to the Lord? Do you pray for *the knowledge of God's will*? For *wisdom and understanding so that you may live a life worthy of the Lord*? (Let's be sure to incorporate these!)

Prayer is not an obligation. It is an awesome privilege and opportunity to intimately converse with our loving Lord and Creator. Prayer is a blessing that we don't want to miss out on—it is a chance to enter God's Holy Presence and spend some quality time with Him. Prayer is an occasion when we step into the Lord's welcoming embrace and pour out our hearts to our Father who cares and listens. Prayer invites the wisdom, power, and authority of God into our situations.

30. How will this perspective motivate you to pray more eagerly and regularly?

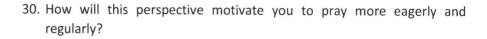

"Do not be anxious about anything, but in every situation, by prayer and petition,

with thanksgiving, present your requests to God." Philippians 4:6

Paul leaves us a great example: through his words we are encouraged to pray for *a knowledge of God's will*, and for *spiritual wisdom and understanding* on how to apply it. With our *minds set on things above* we are more apt to live in a way that pleases and honors the Lord. The fruit of our faith and God's wisdom from above will be clearly evidenced in our lives. With His perspective, we will not fret, panic, and despair; instead, we will be filled with confidence, courage, love, peace, hope, and even joy on all occasions. We will choose truth, righteousness, and compassion. So you see, praying for godly wisdom affects everything!

Throughout this study we will come to see the importance of our thoughts and realize the power that they hold. We are what we think—the meditations of our minds and the focus of our hearts will ultimately direct our lives. An anxious, negative, *the sky is falling mentality,* will bring us to a standstill and hold us in bondage from all the blessings God wants to pour into our lives. We must purposefully *choose* to focus on the Lord and allow Him to transform our mindset.

31. Please read **Proverbs 3:1-8** and record the actions we are encouraged to take and the blessings we incur as a result.

Know that God is at work in you and for you. His ways are always best, His intentions are always good, and His plans are always perfect. Turn to His Word for all the wisdom, understanding, and guidance you need.

"My son, if you accept my words and store up my commands within you, turning your ear to wisdom and applying your heart to understanding— indeed, if you call out for insight and cry aloud for understanding, and if you look for it as for silver and search for it as for hidden treasure, then you will understand the fear of the LORD and find the knowledge of God." Proverbs 2:1-5

32. Read **1 Corinthians 1:25** and jot down the source of true *wisdom* and *strength*. How have you personally experienced this sentiment?

God's wisdom and strength are treasures that are definitely worth pursuing!

Joyful Thanks

Colossians 1:11-14, *"being strengthened with all power according to his glorious might so that you may have great endurance and patience, ¹² and giving joyful thanks to the Father, who has qualified you to share in the inheritance of his holy people in the kingdom of light. ¹³ For he has rescued us from the dominion of darkness and brought us into the kingdom of the Son he loves, ¹⁴ in whom we have redemption, the forgiveness of sins."*

33. What does *endurance* mean to you? How does focusing on the Lord help you patiently endure difficult situations? How does His power help fortify your spirit? Are you able to give *joyful thanks* despite circumstances?

34. Please open your Bible and read **James 1:2-4**, making note of what *perseverance* accomplishes in our lives.

"But you, man of God, flee from all this, and pursue righteousness, godliness, faith, love, endurance, and gentleness. [12] Fight the good fight of the faith. Take hold of the eternal life to which you were called when you made your good confession in the presence of many witnesses." 1 Timothy 6:11-12

35. We have been showered with blessing upon blessing. **Colossians 1:11-14** details the eternal blessings that the Lord has bestowed on us. Slowly reread one verse at a time and savor the extravagant favor God has shown to us. Now write each spiritual benefit we have been given and prayerfully give thanks to your generous Father above. (Keeping these blessings in mind will better equip you to patiently endure in the future.)

"For the LORD God is a sun and shield; the LORD bestows favor and honor; no good thing does he withhold from those whose walk is blameless." Psalm 84:11

36. Please read the following verses and make note of any further information you find regarding your spiritual blessings.

- **Ephesians 1:3-8**

- **Ephesians 1:18-20**

37. Are you filled with joy at all the Lord has done for you? Are you living as an overcomer considering your spiritual blessings? Are you thriving as a conqueror through *Christ who gives you strength* (Philippians 4:13)? Or are you trying to muster the might all on your own? Contemplate these questions and elaborate.

Reflect on your spiritual blessings often—your salvation, Jesus' Presence with you every day, your access to your Heavenly Father, His mighty power at work within you, your eternal place in God's perfect Kingdom of light—a place where all fears, pain, and suffering will be no more. Notice the difference in your perspective and daily life.

We are what we think! So, let's think on the blessings and promises of God! Let's place our hope firmly in Him and praise Him, even amidst our storms!

"The LORD is my strength and my shield; my heart trusts in him, and he helps me.

My heart leaps for joy, and with my song I praise him." Psalm 28:7

Throughout Paul's prayer in Colossians, we are encouraged to *reflect on, remember, trust in, meditate on, bear in mind, contemplate, consider, think about, and know* God's glorious Word. We must deliberately put our hope in Him and praise Him every day! This theme is woven across our study.

38. Please lookup the following verses and record your takeaway lessons.

- **Psalm 103:1-5**

- **Ephesians 1:11-14**

- **1 Peter 1:3-4**

- **2 Corinthians 10:5**

- **Ephesians 4:14**

Knowing that our hope is in Christ guards us against false hopes and the empty promises of the world.

In closing, here are a handful of action steps we can put into practice as *we take our thoughts captive and make them obedient to Christ*:

1. Reflect on your first encounter with Jesus. Think about your daily encounters with Him.

2. Remember your identity in Christ—loved, chosen, forgiven, saved, set free, abundantly blessed.

3. Trust in God your Father. Meditate on His amazing grace and be washed in His unshakeable peace.

4. Bear in mind your future hope. Let it impact your faith today and grow your compassion for others now.

5. Contemplate His grace towards you and offer grace to others.

6. Consider His generous love for you. Allow it to wash over you and change your heart.

7. Know that God is at work for you, in you, and through you. His way is best. Turn to His Word for all the wisdom and understanding you need.

8. Think about your spiritual blessings—your salvation, Jesus' Presence with you every day, your access to your Heavenly Father, His mighty power at work within you, your eternal inheritance in God's perfect Kingdom.

"For what you have done I will always praise you in the presence of your faithful people. And I will hope in your name, for your name is good." Psalm 52:9

I hope this lesson has filled your mind and heart with the hope of Jesus. I pray that it springs forth from your life in faith, love, grace, and joyful gratitude!

Above

We have two mindsets from which to choose—yes, there are just two. We can choose to focus solely on all that immediately surrounds us, or we can lift our eyes to heaven and see the world through the broad lens of eternity. Each vision brings with it a perspective unique in its view. Focusing only on earth and all that it holds reveals a very limited perspective, binding us to the "here and now" with little hope on the horizon. By raising our sights and setting our hearts on Jesus and on the things *above*, our lives become filled with hope of exponential potential, of all that can possibly be. Eyes just on the *world* can bring feelings of ever-searching emptiness. Eyes on *above* ushers deep abiding joy, peace, contentment, and hope. *Above* motivates our thinking, passions, pursuits, actions, and dreams with fresh enthusiasm, purpose, and means. *Above* is where our hope is found, with the heavenly purpose of bringing hope into the world all around us.

"Since, then, you have been raised with Christ, set your hearts on things above, where Christ is, seated at the right hand of God. ² Set your minds on things above, not on earthly things." Colossians 3:1-2

How does an *above* directed mindset help you to overcome, push through, and persevere?

Healthy Diet

You have most likely heard the phrase, *"You are what you eat."* This simply means that whatever we put into our mouths will ultimately affect our bodies. If junk food is our main source of sustenance, then we will begin to feel sluggish and tired, our pants will get tighter as our waist expands, and the glow will fade from our cheeks. If on the other hand, we feast on fruits and veggies and healthier choices; then we will feel more energetic, we'll have more spring in our step, and our eyes will be brighter.

The same is true of our minds: *"We are what we think."* If we allow our minds to constantly be filled with the negativity of this world, the division of politics, and the angry voices that are all around us, then we are more likely to experience anxiety and depression. If we ruminate on the doubts, worries, and fears that infiltrate our thoughts, allowing them to have full reign, we will most likely feel overwhelmed, discouraged, negative, and hopeless. If the news and social media are the mainstays of our mental diet, then the joy of the Lord will be stolen from our hearts and the peace of God will be snatched from our lives.

As vital as it is for us to consume a healthy diet for our bodies, it is even more essential for our minds. We must consciously grab hold of our thoughts and refocus our minds onto the Word of God—it is filled with amazing promises. *He will never leave us or forsake* us (Deuteronomy 31:8). *He is our strong tower* (Proverbs 18:10). *He is our refuge in times of trouble* (Psalm 46:1). *He is our Living Water* (John 4:13-14). God is loving and all-powerful, and we are *His beloved children* (Galatians 3:26). Let's feast our minds on the infallible truths of Scripture! It is the only way to remain satisfied and unshaken!

"We are what we think"—Let's fill our minds with God's Word until there is no more room for lies and discouragement to sneak in.

What damaging ingredients have you been feeding your mind thus far?

How can feasting your mind on God's Truth help you enjoy a healthier life?

Lookup the previous Scripture references to be satisfied with good things!

"Within your temple, O God, we meditate on your unfailing love. Like your name, O God, your praise reaches to the ends of the earth; your right hand is filled with righteousness."

Psalm 48:9-10

Christ is Supreme

Colossians 1:15-2:3

How often does your mind wander into places it should not go? How often do your thoughts get stuck on things that are simply no good for you? If you're anything like me, it's far too often. The future *what ifs* and the urgency of the *here and now* sometimes press in and eclipse my view of my all-powerful, loving Heavenly Father. Fortunately, there is hope for both our wayward minds. The Bible says to counteract our worries, fears, regrets, and worldly distractions, by purposefully choosing to focus on the Lord daily, allowing Him to redirect our thoughts to where they belong. We must *set our hearts and minds on things above where Christ is* seated on the throne in complete authority!

Let's remember this: our help comes from the Lord, Maker of Heaven and Earth! This lesson covers **Colossians 1:15-2:3** and reminds us to seek and find rest in Christ's supreme and sovereign character. To *rest in God's character*, we must first familiarize ourselves with the attributes of His character.

1. From what you already know about God, how would you describe Him to someone else? How would you explain who Jesus is?

Colossians gives us great insight into the divine nature of God, as revealed through His Son, Jesus Christ. My prayer is that you come away from this lesson with a greater understanding of both God the Father and Jesus Christ the Son.

Please begin by reading our whole portion of Scripture, **Colossians 1:15-2:3.** These Scriptures answer three foundational questions for us—Who is Jesus Christ? What does He show us regarding God the Father? What has He accomplished for us?

We will now break down our passage into smaller nuggets of truth and allow them to saturate our minds. Before going any further in our lesson, pause, pray, and ask God to give you a revelation of Himself, by knowing His Son Jesus more intimately through His Word.

Exact Representation

Colossians 1:15, *"The Son is the image of the invisible God, the firstborn over all creation."*

Our God reigns from Heaven above, and His glory is more than our earthly minds can fully comprehend or grasp. God is a God of relationship, and He wants to be known by us. So, He sent His Son Jesus to earth to reveal His nature in a way that we can understand, relate to, and approach. If we want to know what God is like we need only study the life of Jesus as found in the Gospels. Through Jesus' life, we see that God is loving, kind, merciful, gracious, righteous, and holy. He is omnipotent, omnipresent, and sovereign over all of creation. Jesus' teachings, healing, and miracles all point to a God who sees, hears, and cares about us, acting mightily on our behalf. Jesus is the exact image of our invisible God.

Jesus is the Word: "In the beginning was the Word, and the Word was with God, and the Word was God. ² He was with God in the beginning. ³ Through him all things were made; without him nothing was made that has been made. ⁴ In him was life, and that life was the light of all mankind. ⁵ The light shines in the darkness, and the darkness has not overcome it." John 1:1-5

"The Son is the radiance of God's glory and the exact representation of his being, sustaining all things by his powerful word." Hebrews 1:3

2. What do you learn about Jesus' identity from these additional verses? How is Jesus described? What has He accomplished and what does He continue to do?

Jesus is a revelation of who God is; the Bible is a revelation of who Jesus is. He created everything in heaven and on earth. At His Word all things came into being and every living creature sprang to life. He alone reigns supreme over all creation—He holds authority over life, death, and all of eternity. Although Jesus is the King of kings and has all of heaven and earth under His control, He humbled Himself and came to this earth to fulfill the Father's plan—giving His life to gain our salvation. Jesus shows us what it looks like to live surrendered to our Heavenly Father (Matt 26:36-42). Jesus is the manifestation of God's glory in the flesh; God's children—you and I—are called to conform to the image of Jesus by submitting to the Father and shining the light of His glory too.

3. Read the following verses and make note of how God is at work in us as we wait for Jesus' return. (Praise the Lord, He is coming back!)

   • **Romans 8:28-30**

   • **Ephesians 4:23-24; 5:1-2, 8**

4. What is God's goal for us? How can aligning our lives to His will bring us a deeper, lasting joy? How have you personally experienced this?

5. Faith, humility, obedience, righteousness, holiness, love, goodness, and truth are what God desires. In what ways and areas would you like your life to reflect Jesus' life and character better? Ask God to help you.

Created Through Him

Colossians 1:16, *"For in him all things were created: things in heaven and on earth, visible and invisible, whether thrones or powers or rulers or authorities; all things have been created through him and for him. "*

6. Read the following verses and underline or highlight all references to God's creation and His matchless authority over it:

- **Genesis, 1:1**, "In the beginning God created the heavens and the earth."

- **Genesis 1:21**, "So God created the great creatures of the sea and every living thing with which the water teems and that moves about in it, according to their kinds, and every winged bird according to its kind. And God saw that it was good."

- **Genesis 1:27**, "So God created mankind in his own image, in the image of God he created them; male and female he created them."

- **John 1:3**, "Through him all things were made; without him nothing was made that has been made."

- **Philippians 2:8-11** ESV, "And being found in human form, he humbled himself by becoming obedient to the point of death, even death on a cross. [9] Therefore God has highly exalted him and bestowed on him the name that is above every name, [10] so that at the name of Jesus every knee should bow, in heaven and on earth and under the earth, [11] and every tongue confess that Jesus Christ is Lord, to the glory of God the Father."

- **Hebrews 11:3**, "By faith we understand that the universe was formed at God's command, so that what is seen was not made out of what was visible."

7. Reflect on these verses and summarize what you learned. List everything that is under God's authority.

God created all things on this earth: the plants, animals, humans, water, and land. He is Creator of everything in the heavens: the atmosphere, the sky, the stars, the moon, the sun, the galaxies near and far away. He created angels who serve Him, and even Satan and the angels-turned-demons who went astray. There is nothing outside of His Divine authority, and Jesus' death and resurrection prove it! Every knee will ultimately bow in reverence before Him!

If God was able to create the universe out of nothing, surely, He can create a new heart inside of us. He is sovereign over absolutely everything. He lovingly *knit and wove* you together inside your mother's womb (Psalm 139). Trust the supreme and holy character of God to cleanse your heart and renew your spirit today.

"Create in me a clean heart, O God, and renew a right spirit within me." Psalm 51:10

_____

"Forget the former things; do not dwell on the past. [19] See, I am doing a new thing! Now it springs up; do you not perceive it? I am making a way in the wilderness and streams in the wasteland." Isaiah 43:18-19

8. What *new thing* do you need the Lord to do in your life currently? Write a prayer asking Him to *cleanse your heart, renew your spirit, spring forth, and make a way* for you today.

Dear Lord,

Amen.

Holds Together

Colossians 1:17, *"He is before all things, and in him all things hold together."*

9. Lookup the following verses and write them out in the spaces provided. This will help solidify God's Word in your mind.

- **Psalm 102:25**

- **Hebrews 1:3**

The Lord not only created the earth, but He also sustains it day after day. He not only created your life, but He also sustains you moment by moment.

10. Do you feel Him holding you together today? Do you trust Him with your life and situation? Elaborate.

"Who has gone up to heaven and come down? Whose hands have gathered up the wind? Who has wrapped up the waters in a cloak? Who has established all the ends of the earth? What is his name, and what is the name of his son? Surely you know!"

Proverbs 30:4

He is the Head

Colossians 1:18, *"And he is the head of the body, the church; he is the beginning and the firstborn from among the dead, so that in everything he might have the supremacy."*

In addition to being the Creator and Sustainer of you and me and the whole planet; Jesus is the head of the worldwide church, past, present, and future. Without Him there would be no church at all. People such as pastors, preachers, and teachers are not the head of the church, they are only stewards and ministers of the Gospel. The church exists because of Jesus and is built upon Him only! His resurrection from the grave was the catalyst of the church and it is the foundation of our faith. Jesus was the first to be raised from the dead into glory, and we get to victoriously follow His lead when He returns for us someday. He is supreme over our lives from now through eternity! At His death on the Cross our sin was completely paid for, and because of His resurrection we gain the hope of resurrection too. He gave us breath on the day of our birth. He gives us the Holy Spirit at the moment of our salvation. Our lives bear witness to the power and truth of the Gospel Message. Jesus is the firstborn of all creation; He was the first One to experience resurrected life and ascend to be with the Father in Heaven. Because of His sacrifice, we will someday step into glory and be with Him.

11. Please read **Revelation 1:4-8** and note any additional words on Jesus being *firstborn* and what it accomplishes for us. How do these verses affirm and encourage your faith in Jesus?

12. Please read the following Scriptures and record what you find regarding the promises of our resurrection in Christ.

- **1 Thessalonians 4:13-18**

- **1 Corinthians 15:20-23**

- **Romans 6:5**

- **1 Peter 1:3-4**

"Blessed and holy are those who share in the first resurrection. The second death has no power over them, but they will be priests of God and of Christ and will reign with him for a thousand years." Revelation 20:6

We do not need to fear death because Jesus has promised us eternal life with Him. He has also promised that we will have new resurrected bodies and minds, better suited to last for eternity. We will no longer be burdened with aches and pains, regrets and shame, heartbreak and sorrows. We will never again be tormented by sin or bear its lingering effects. We will be new creations, dwelling in a new heaven and new earth! How amazing is that!

13. How does the hope of the resurrection affect you right now?

All His Fullness

Colossians 1:19, *"For God was pleased to have all his fullness dwell in him,"*

14. Please read the following Scriptures and note the affirmations as to the fullness of God in Jesus. Absolutely nothing is lacking. Jesus is Lord.

- **John 10:30**

- **John 10:38**

- **John 12:49-50**

"Anyone who welcomes you welcomes me, and anyone who welcomes me welcomes the one who sent me." Matthew 10:40

Jesus Christ is God in the flesh. When He walked this earth, He was both fully human and fully divine. He is the manifestation of God among us. Before His birth the angel proclaimed that Jesus was to be called Immanuel, which means, *"God with us."* (Matthew 1:23)

God's fullness dwells in Jesus; Jesus came to dwell among men. How beautiful and reassuring to know that God loves us so much that He left Heaven's Throne Room to show us the way back to Himself. And He continues to be with us every day. He has sent His Holy Spirit to dwell within us. We have continual fellowship with the Holy Trinity.

"Do not fear, for I Am with you." Isaiah 41:10

———————

"Be strong and courageous. The Lord goes with you wherever you go." Joshua 1:9

15. How does the knowledge that *God is with you* strengthen your heart?

16. Jesus walked this earth fully human, and He personally experienced the effects of this broken world; He can empathize with our troubles and weaknesses. What comfort does this bring you? Being that He is fully God, He has the power to move on our behalf. How does this knowledge encourage you?

We can rest in the character of God because Jesus has shown us how exceedingly faithful, merciful, gracious, loving, patient, powerful, and sovereign He is!

We have studied who Jesus is; now we will look at what He has attained for us.

He Reconciles

Colossians 1:20-22, *"and through him to reconcile to himself all things, whether things on earth or things in heaven, by making peace through his blood, shed on the cross. ²¹ Once you were alienated from God and were enemies in your minds because of your evil behavior. ²² But now he has reconciled you by Christ's physical body through death to present you holy in his sight, without blemish and free from accusation—"*

17. Please read the following verses for a deeper understanding of the *reconciliation* Jesus brings between us and God the Father. Underline or highlight all the benefits you receive from Jesus.

- **Romans 5:10**, "For if, while we were God's enemies, we were reconciled to him through the death of his Son, how much more, having been reconciled, shall we be saved through his life!"

- **Romans 8:33-39**, "Who will bring any charge against those whom God has chosen? It is God who justifies. ³⁴ Who then is the one who condemns? No one. Christ Jesus who died—more than that, who was raised to life—is at the right hand of God and is also interceding for us. ³⁵ Who shall separate us from the love of Christ? Shall trouble or hardship or persecution or famine or nakedness or danger or sword? ³⁶ As it is written: 'For your sake we face death all day long; we are considered as sheep to be slaughtered.' ³⁷ No, in all these things we are more than conquerors through him who loved us. ³⁸ For I am convinced that neither death nor life, neither angels nor demons, neither the present nor the future, nor any powers, ³⁹ neither height nor depth, nor anything else in all creation, will be able to separate us from the love of God that is in Christ Jesus our Lord."

- **Jude 1:24,** "To him who is able to keep you from stumbling and to present you before his glorious presence without fault and with great joy—"

18. Look back over **Colossians 1:20-22** and the previous verses. Slowly savor their words of hope and promise. Now take a moment to summarize in your own words the blessings that Jesus pours out on your life and what it means to you.

Having been reconciled to God through Jesus' death on the Cross is not something to be taken lightly. Jesus endured torture, ridicule, denial, persecution, and death on our behalf, all with the purpose of canceling our debt, freeing us from the shackles of sin, and giving us the hope of eternal life. There is only one logical response we can have: to take up our cross and live for Him daily. This means turning from sin and pursuing righteousness. (We'll study this more in a future lesson.)

19. I think now would be the perfect time to read the story of Jesus' death and resurrection. All four Gospels record these momentous events. Please choose one of the following narratives for an eye opening, heart-wrenching, joy-inspiring account of Jesus' most significant days on earth: **Matthew 26, 27, 28; Mark 14, 15, 16; Luke 22, 23, 24; John 18, 19, 20**.

Record your thoughts here:

- Jesus' words and actions at the Last Supper:

- Regarding His friends' treatment of Him:

- During His time in the Garden of Gethsemane:

- When brought before the religious leaders:

- While standing before Pilate:

- The soldiers' mockery and abuse of Him:

- At His death on the Cross:

- At His glorious resurrection:

What a rollercoaster of emotions. From Friday to Sunday our hearts range from overwhelming sorrow, fear, and defeat to extraordinary joy, gratitude, and celebration. Jesus' death and resurrection are the bridge to our reconciliation with God and the key to our canceled debt and eternal hope.

20. Describe your emotions as you read the Good Friday and Easter story.

From the time of Creation, we were made to be in relationship with God. Adam and Eve walked and talked freely with God in the Garden of Eden, until they disobeyed the Lord and took a bite of the forbidden fruit. At that moment, sin entered in and caused division between God and mankind. Our waywardness was no surprise to God. He always had a way to restore and reconcile us to Himself—the Cross was always His plan (Gen 3:15). God promised to send a Savior to be a sacrifice for our sin, taking the punishment we deserve. By Jesus' death and our faith in Him, we now stand holy and blameless, above reproach before His Throne—instead of judgment, we find grace. We are reconciled to God through Jesus' death on the Cross. He is our peace; He justifies us; He Intercedes for us. He is supreme over our salvation. He makes us more than conquerors and promises that nothing can ever separate us from His lavish love (Rom 8:37-39).

21. If Jesus is supreme over everything, why do we so often behave like He isn't? Do you believe that God is bigger than your problems? Are you acting like it? Is there an area of your life where you especially struggle to remember that Christ is Lord?

22. Do you tend to rely on your own self-sufficiency, or do you surrender and trust the sufficiency of Jesus' power? Put your thoughts into words:

23. What specific problems do you need to lay at Jesus' feet? Pause now and ask God to help you trust Him and hand your cares, concerns, and circumstances over to His capable care.

We know God's character and we believe that He has reconciled us to Himself through Jesus' sacrifice on the Cross. Now we'll look at how our salvation should impact our lives. In the following verses we will read what God's heart and will is for His children.

Full Riches

Colossians 1:23-2:3, *"if you continue in your faith, established and firm, and do not move from the hope held out in the gospel. This is the gospel that you heard and that has been proclaimed to every creature under heaven, and of which I, Paul, have become a servant.*

[24] Now I rejoice in what I am suffering for you, and I fill up in my flesh what is still lacking in regard to Christ's afflictions, for the sake of his body, which is the church. [25] I have become its servant by the commission God gave me to present to you the word of God in its fullness— [26] the mystery that has been kept hidden for ages and generations, but is now disclosed to the Lord's people. [27] To them God has chosen to make known among the Gentiles the glorious riches of this mystery, which is Christ in you, the hope of glory.

[28] He is the one we proclaim, admonishing and teaching everyone with all wisdom, so that we may present everyone fully mature in Christ. [29] To this end I strenuously contend with all the energy Christ so powerfully works in me.

[2:1] I want you to know how hard I am contending for you and for those at Laodicea, and for all who have not met me personally. [2] My goal is that they may be encouraged in heart and united in love, so that they may have the full riches of complete understanding, in order that they may know the mystery of God, namely, Christ, [3] in whom are hidden all the treasures of wisdom and knowledge."

24. Reread this passage two or three times and make note of what stands out to you. What comfort and encouragement do you gain? What exhortation do you hear?

Through Christ, we have indeed been given the *full riches of complete understanding*. Jesus gives us revelation of God's heart, motive, and purpose. He reveals God's abundant love, mercy, and grace.

25. Paul says that the glorious "*mystery* of God is *Christ in us, the hope of glory*." It is truly remarkable that when we place our faith in Jesus as our Lord and Savior His Holy Spirit personally comes to dwell in our hearts through faith! The Holy Spirit is described as our comforter, encourager, teacher, advocate, and guide. He seals us for the Day of Redemption, proving we have a place in Heaven. What does this blessing mean to you?

Fullness, riches, all-sufficient, complete, everything—all words that beautifully describe our Lord and Savior Jesus Christ. He is the Lord of lords and King of kings. He came from Heaven to earth to teach us about His Heavenly Kingdom; He gave His life to pay for our sins; He rose from the grave to give us new life. He takes up residence in our hearts, renews our minds, and gives us His Holy Spirit, equipping us with everything we need for pursuing godly lives. (2 Peter 1:3)

As Jesus hung on the Cross He uttered these words, "*It is finished!*" (John 19:30) He fully and finally accomplished our salvation. Nothing more is needed, but for us to *confess with our mouths that Jesus is Lord and believe in our hearts that He was raised from the dead, and we will be saved.* (Romans 10:9) We cannot do anything to earn our salvation and we cannot lose our salvation once we place our lives firmly and securely in the Father's hand. (John 10:28-29)

In his letter to the Colossians, Paul reminds them and us, that Christ is sufficient for all our needs. We can cease our endless searching and instead rest our hearts in the capable care of our Savior and fix our minds on His heavenly promises. Instead of hoping that power, money, influence, popularity, relationships, success, and even busyness will fill the void in our lives, we can confidently come to Jesus and allow Him to fill our souls in a way that nothing and no one else can. He showers us in unconditional love, kindness, and goodness. He fills us with unshakable faith, hope, peace, and joy. He strengthens us and equips us with His mighty power. Jesus is God's glorious *mystery* revealed to humanity!

26. Please open your Bible and read the following verses for confirmation that Jesus is supreme. Make note of all the ways that He is sufficient in supplying our needs.

- **Isaiah 43:10-11**

- **John 1:16-18**

- **2 Corinthians 12:9**

- **Ephesians 3:16-21**

"And my God will meet all your needs according to the riches of his glory in Christ Jesus." Philippians 4:19

When Paul stated, *"I will fill up in my flesh what is still lacking in regard to Christ's afflictions, for the sake of his body, which is the church,"* (v.24) he was in no way saying that more was needed to make Christ's sacrifice sufficient. He was merely proclaiming that he, and we, have a part to play in response to all that Jesus accomplished for us. We must take up our cross and follow Him; we must lay down our life for Jesus and go where He leads us (Matthew 16:24). We must live to love, pursue, serve, and glorify God and to proclaim the Good News of the Gospel. We must not grow weary in our faith but lean into Jesus and *"strenuously contend with all the energy Christ so powerfully works in us."* (v.29)

27. How does Christ's supremacy and sufficiency hearten and fortify you? How does setting your mind on Him help you to *continue in your faith, established and firm*?

28. I have three final verses for you to lookup for our lesson this week. Please record what you find regarding God, Christ, and our purpose and motivation. What does this mean to you personally?

   • **Hebrews 9:14**

   • **1 Timothy 6:12-16**

   • **Acts 17:24-28**

Continue in your faith, lean in, and press on. Don't be swayed from the hope of the Gospel, which is *Christ in you*! Don't be led astray by doubts, insecurities, and false teachings of Christ's insufficiency. He is enough—He is all we need. *"For in him we live and move and have our being."* Let's determine to be firm in our beliefs, rooted and established, continually maturing in our faith. Let's grab hold of all the treasures of wisdom and knowledge made available to us in Christ.

In Him

God is the source of all our life. Everything we have emanates from Him—Our physical life, our spiritual life, our eternal life, and our abundant life are all found in Him alone.

God fills our lungs with life-giving oxygen on the day of our birth. He fills us with His life-changing Holy Spirit on the day of our salvation. He invites us into His Heavenly Kingdom to dwell with Him forever. He pours out endless blessings as we reside here on the earth. In Him we find our real identity—we are children of the Most High God; we are royalty. We are saved, redeemed, forgiven, and set free. In God alone, we find our purpose and reason for living. He is the source of our confidence, our hope, our peace, our joy, and our strength. If we ever find ourselves running on empty, it's because we've gone rogue and are trying to do it all alone! We must surrender our body, mind, and spirit, our present and future to His capable hands.

In the outstretched arms of our Savior, we encounter the fullest expression of sacrificial love, and an invitation to experience life in all its glory. I encourage you to lean into the Lord more and more each day and draw strength from Him with every aspect of your being.

"He is before all things, and in him all things hold together." Colossians 1:17

Let's set our minds on the supremacy of Christ over this world and His sovereignty in our lives. Let's close our lesson by coming before the Lord in prayer:

Lord, You are sovereign over the day and night, over the dark and the light, over things seen and unseen to our naked eyes. You are in complete control over everything. Thank you, Lord, that we can rest in Your omnipotent care and find refuge in Your holy Presence. There is nothing taking place on this planet of which You are not acutely aware. Thank you, God, for never leaving or forsaking us, even on our wayward days. The world may seem in chaos, but You are in control, You are good, and that never changes. You are with us amid our circumstances, trials, tribulations, and our celebrations. Our hope, peace, and joy cannot be shaken, so long as we trust in You. Thank You, Jesus. Amen.

"One generation commends your works to another;

they tell of your mighty acts.

They speak of the glorious splendor of your majesty—

and I will meditate on your wonderful works.

They tell of the power of your awesome works—

and I will proclaim your great deeds."

Psalm 145:4-6

Fullness in Christ

Colossians 2:4-23

I am so excited for you to grasp the concepts in this lesson! You and I have been brought to *fullness* through our union with the Lord. God is the great I AM, and He chose to dwell among humanity in the person of Jesus Christ. He is self-existent, needing no one and nothing to sustain Him, and yet He sought out a relationship with us. He created the heavens and the earth out of void and emptiness; He created mankind in His own image for the distinct purpose of reflecting His glory. Our previous lesson established Christ's supremacy in all things. He is sufficient for all our needs, and in Him alone we find our true identity!

We are children of the Most High God who reigns from His Throne Room in Heaven above. We are sons and daughters of the Mighty King—we are royalty!

But do we live according to this reality? Unfortunately, not always.

1. How can these truths about God's sovereignty and your identity in Christ reframe your mindset and help you find confidence today?

Having written both a Bible study and devotional dedicated exclusively to this topic, know that I am deeply passionate about helping women and men embrace their God-given identity and discover the full riches that are found in Christ. It is the only way for us to remain unshaken in this topsy-turvy world. This lesson will dive deep into this message and will hopefully help us lift our eyes to Heaven and set our minds firmly on the truth of who God says we are.

Last week we discussed the amazing character of God as revealed through Jesus Christ. We were reminded that He is Lord of all creation and is sovereign over absolutely everything—past, present, and future! We established *who He is*, and we reflected on *all He has done for us* through His death and resurrection. He has *reconciled us to Himself* and *presents us holy and free from accusation*. Our lesson closed with an exhortation to *continue in our faith, established and firm*.

As a refresher let's read Colossians 2:2-3 from last week.

Colossians 2:2-3, *"My goal is that they may be encouraged in heart and united in love, so that they may have the <u>full riches</u> of complete understanding, in order that they may know the mystery of God, namely, Christ,* [3] *in whom are hidden <u>all the treasures</u> of wisdom and knowledge."*

2. How have the *full riches* of personally knowing Jesus changed your perspective? How is your heart being encouraged, even possibly in the face of difficulties?

3. How are *all the treasures of wisdom and knowledge,* which are found in Christ, impacting your life, and helping to guide your steps each day?

Our lesson today takes up right where Paul's letter left off and builds on his previous statement. We will now take a closer look at *who we are in Christ*.

4. Please read **Colossians 2:4-23** for an overview of our lesson. Jot down a few notes regarding your observations.

Rooted and Built Up

Colossians 2:4-8, *"I tell you this so that no one may deceive you by fine-sounding arguments. ⁵ For though I am absent from you in body, I am present with you in spirit and delight to see how disciplined you are and how firm your faith in Christ is. ⁶ So then, just as you received Christ Jesus as Lord, continue to live your lives in him, ⁷ rooted and built up in him, strengthened in the faith as you were taught, and overflowing with thankfulness. ⁸ See to it that no one takes you captive through hollow and deceptive philosophy, which depends on human tradition and the elemental spiritual forces of this world rather than on Christ."*

There is no greater knowledge than the knowledge of Jesus Christ. The mystery of God is unwrapped and revealed in Him alone. The entire Old Testament pointed to Him as our coming Savior. In Him we find understanding of God's plan for this world and our place in it. Through our relationship with Jesus Christ, we discover our purpose for our time here on earth—to know and glorify God with our lives and draw near to Him as His beloved son or daughter. Everything makes sense when we see life through the lens of God's eternal plan. We know that there is an absolute beginning and an assured glorious end. God created the world, and He created humanity; He made and executed a plan to save you and me. Jesus went to the Cross and gave His life to pay the penalty for our sin and reconcile us to our Heavenly Father. We are saved by faith in the grace of God alone—not by working hard enough, not through philosophies, religions, rules, or traditions. God took all the guess work and uncertainty out of the equation. He did all the work necessary for us to be made right with Him. There is nothing we can add to our salvation to make it better or more secure. Christ is all we need. The same Gospel we placed our faith in is the same one we must *continue in.* We must be rooted and established in the foundational truths of the Gospel, so that we are not easily persuaded or moved away from them. God's Word must be the foundation, the framework, and the holy standard on which we build our lives.

5. Are you ever tempted to strive to earn your salvation by working hard or being good enough? How does God's gift of grace lift the burden from your shoulders and free you to enjoy your relationship with Him?

Our salvation is instantaneous, but our faith is not a one-and-done; it is a continual work in progress. We must grow in our relationship with the Lord, by tending to our faith—we cannot neglect or forget it, otherwise it will become dry and lifeless. We must be grounded in His love and built up in His divine power; always drawing refreshment and direction from His Word, seeking refuge in His arms, regularly coming to Him in prayer, and finding protection in His Presence.

The world offers a wide array of alternatives to the One True God. There are various religions to choose from, ranging from eastern spirituality and practices to western celebrity idolatry. People mistakenly worship and pray to angels and saints. Some even worship the devil who is destined for hell. People idolize other humans, themselves, and even manmade gods carved with their own two hands. A few years ago, I traveled to Jordan and Israel. While in Jordan we visited the world-famous Petra with its narrow gorge that leads to an ancient city formerly occupied by people called the Nabateans. As we walked through the gorge, we noticed carvings along the way. One such carving was a stone block with two eyes etched on the side—there was no mouth opening. We asked our guide about this object. He said it was one of the gods that the people used to worship. It had no mouth because the god did not speak. Left to our own imaginations, it's astonishing and heartbreaking the lengths people will go to and the things that humans will come up with to worship—a lifeless block of stone among them. Fortunately, we have a God who speaks—He has given us the Bible as a means of communication. He invites us to pray as a means of relationship. There is no need to search any further.

6. What various philosophies and traditions are you familiar with? Do they counteract the teachings of Scripture by adding to Jesus or subtracting from His power, authority, and words in any way?

Stand firm on what the Bible teaches about God and regarding your identity—don't let anyone sway you from the glorious truth. Confidently and respectfully encourage others to stay faithful to the one true God too.

7. Reading your Bible is the best way to ensure not falling victim to false teachings. By knowing the truth according to God's Word, you and I will more readily recognize the lies. How is Bible study helping you more effectively guard against lies and false teachings?

8. I love the way Paul laid out some essentials for our faith in verses **2:6-8**. Read through the following phrases and record your thoughts on each. How can, or do you, personally implement each practice in your own life?

- *You received Christ Jesus as Lord*

- *Continue to live your lives in him*

- *Be rooted and built up in him*

- *Be strengthened in the faith as you were taught*

- *Be overflowing with thankfulness*

- *See to it that no one takes you captive through hollow and deceptive philosophy*

9. Please read the following verses and answer the related questions.

- **Ephesians 3:17**—What does Paul want us to be *rooted and established in*? Why do you think this is so important for us?

- **2 Peter 1:3-13**—What does Peter desire that we are *established in* (1:12)? What qualities does Peter exhort us to *possess in increasing measure* (1:5-7)? For what reason?

10. I'm almost positive I know your answer, but I'm going to ask anyway with the purpose of having you reflect on the question: Would you rather stumble into the Kingdom when Jesus returns, or grab hold of His hand and walk confidently in beside Him? Explain.

If we are already in the practice of walking in rhythm closely with Jesus here on earth, then stepping into His Kingdom will be a seamless transition in our journey.

Keep your faith fresh by abiding in Jesus and simply enjoying your relationship with Him. Renew your faith continually by reflecting on and remembering the truths found in Christ. Let Him be your companion and guide for your life.

"They will be like a tree planted by the water that sends out its roots by the stream. It does not fear when heat comes; its leaves are always green. It has no worries in a year of drought and never fails to bear fruit." Jeremiah 17:8

11. Are you sinking your roots into Jesus? How does He spiritually sustain and refresh you even during emotionally and physically dry seasons?

12. Please read **Matthew 13:18-23** and record what you learn regarding the various soil types and how they respond to the seeds.

13. How does good soil provide the perfect environment for growing deep roots? How can this ensure that you don't fall away during times of trouble? What actions or disciplines are you putting into practice to prepare your heart and help your roots grow?

Raised with Him

Colossians 2:9-15, *"For in Christ all the fullness of the Deity lives in bodily form, [10] and in Christ you have been brought to fullness. He is the head over every power and authority. [11] In him you were also circumcised with a circumcision not performed by human hands. Your whole self ruled by the flesh was put off when you were circumcised by Christ, [12] having been buried with him in baptism, in which you were also raised with him through your faith in the working of God, who raised him from the dead. [13] When you were dead in your sins and in the uncircumcision of your flesh, God made you alive with Christ. He forgave us all our sins, [14] having canceled the charge of our legal indebtedness, which stood against us and condemned us; he has taken it away, nailing it to the cross. [15] And having disarmed the powers and authorities, he made a public spectacle of them, triumphing over them by the cross."*

The word *"fullness"* grabs my attention in these verses—and I'm sure that was Paul's intent. It stresses the truth that there is absolutely nothing lacking in Jesus, and there is nothing lacking in our identity in Christ. All the fullness of God lives in Jesus—He is the exact representation of Him. He is the fullness of love, hope, peace, and joy. He is the fullness of our salvation—there is nothing more that is needed. We are forgiven solely because of His sacrifice—that's why Jesus said, 'It is finished,' when He hung on the Cross and took His last breath. In Him alone we find our fullness; we are counted as righteous; we find abundant life. He has circumcised our hearts by cutting away our sinful nature, making us more into His image and likeness.

The moment we placed our faith in Him, we were baptized with the Holy Spirit and forever marked with His seal. The act of baptism that we participate in at church is an outward expression of our new life in Christ—dying to sin and being born again; it symbolizes the change that's occurred inside of us and is a public proclamation of our faith. We are God's beloved possession, and we belong to Him eternally. We now get to live for the Lord's glory and shine brightly for Him. Jesus took our sin to the Cross and nailed it there—He paid for it in full. Jesus took away Satan's power over us and removed the threat of death. We are forgiven and made new. When doubts, insecurities, shame, or bitterness try whispering into our ears, we must remember all that Jesus did and accomplished on our behalf and leave the lies at the foot of the Cross—that is right where they belong.

In our day-to-day life we often forget the countless blessings that are ours in Christ. We are meant to be in the world but not of it—the world has no hold over us so long as we remember who we really belong to (John 17:16-17). We are more than conquerors through Christ (Romans 8:37). Nothing can ever separate us from His lavish love. We have been made alive and have been given a place in God's Heavenly Kingdom. We are sealed with His Spirit and His Word is written on our hearts. This is our true identity and the truth we are to meditate on!

14. Are you living in the reality and taking advantage of the fact that you have been brought to fullness and raised to life in Christ? Share examples of what this looks like in your daily life.

15. Please lookup the following verses and make note of everything you discover regarding the blessings incurred through your identity in Christ.

   • **Romans 8:31-39**

   • **Ephesians 2:4-7**

   • **2 Peter 1:2-4**

16. How does this impact your confidence and your view of yourself?

The Reality

Colossians 2:16-19, *"Therefore do not let anyone judge you by what you eat or drink, or with regard to a religious festival, a New Moon celebration or a Sabbath day. [17] These are a shadow of the things that were to come; the reality, however, is found in Christ. [18] Do not let anyone who delights in false humility and the worship of angels disqualify you. Such a person also goes into great detail about what they have seen; they are puffed up with idle notions by their unspiritual mind. [19] They have lost connection with the head, from whom the whole body, supported and held together by its ligaments and sinews, grows as God causes it to grow."*

In Christ we find the reality of all God's plans. Everything in the Old Testament and the days leading up to Jesus' arrival pointed to the time when He would come and fulfill all requirements on our behalf. Previously God had ordained special days for the Jewish people to observe, yearly holidays to celebrate, and certain Laws about food and drink and many other things for them to follow. These were intended to draw the peoples' hearts closer to God and prompt them to seek and worship Him with their lives, and to set them apart from the pagan cultures that surrounded them. (Take a peek at Leviticus.) Sadly, these feasts, special days, ceremonies, and Laws, which were meant to lead the people to worship the LORD, became a burden instead of a joy. Somewhere along the line, the religious leaders began adding their own oppressive laws and laying them on the shoulders of the people. More importance was placed on adhering to the list of rules and regulations than seeking the heart of God. The thinking was that the more rules we follow, the more righteous we'll appear. Sacrifices were offered with fear and pride, rather than humble gratitude. Worship had gotten off track.

But then, God sent Jesus to be the Light of the world. Everything in the Old Testament Scriptures foreshadowed Jesus who fulfills all the requirements on our behalf. In the New Testament, opening with the Gospel of Matthew, there are no more shadows, but we see clearly in the reality and substance of Christ. Jesus sets us apart in the world. The Law is now written on our hearts, it is no longer an outward list of do's and don'ts; by the power of the Holy Spirit, it has become a part of who we are. We don't have to wait for a special religious day to celebrate—every day is a day to rejoice! No matter what day we wake up, we can sincerely proclaim that, *"This is the day that the Lord has made. I will rejoice and be glad in it (Psalm 118:24)."* In Jesus we find our Sabbath rest every single day. We don't have to wait until Sunday service. Whenever we enter His Presence, it is a time of awestruck worship and praise. There is no secret knowledge to approaching God—everything is revealed in Jesus. We must stay connected to Him!

17. Would you rather follow rules and religion in order to please God and secure your place with Him, or would you rather walk with Him in a loving relationship, resting assured that He has already reserved your place in His Kingdom? I'm pretty sure you prefer the latter and I know I do too! Pause and reflect on all the ways you enjoy your relationship with the Lord. What peace does it bring? Record all your thoughts here:

18. Please lookup the following Scriptures and record how Jesus fulfills the Law for us, meeting every requirement on our behalf.

- **Matthew 5:17-18**

- **Hebrews 10:1-10**

- **Ephesians 2:8-9**

19. Do you find that you are still tirelessly striving for perfection through rule following or are you fully resting in all that Jesus fulfilled on your behalf? Or is it a little mix of both? Explain.

Joy and Freedom in Christ

Colossians 2:20-23, *"Since you died with Christ to the elemental spiritual forces of this world, why, as though you still belonged to the world, do you submit to its rules: [21] "Do not handle! Do not taste! Do not touch!"? [22] These rules, which have to do with things that are all destined to perish with use, are based on merely human commands and teachings. [23] Such regulations indeed have an appearance of wisdom, with their self-imposed worship, their false humility and their harsh treatment of the body, but they lack any value in restraining sensual indulgence."*

In addition to correcting the teaching that strict adherence to Jewish Law was essential for salvation, here Paul was addressing certain pagan philosophies and behaviors that were infiltrating the Colossian church and leading people away from the truth of Jesus. Some false teachers within the church were preaching Greek-rooted asceticism and stoicism, which are found nowhere in the Bible. Asceticism teaches abstinence from all worldly pleasures. It promotes a severe form of self-control and harsh discipline to drive sin out. It claims that a person can attain a high spiritual and moral state by practicing self-denial. Stoicism preaches a philosophy that endures pain and is indifferent to pleasure.

Neither of these ideologies fits with the message of Christ. They are human conceptions that put the focus on oneself— *"Look at what I'm doing and see how religious I am."* Seeking glory for ourselves instead of God is not in line with Scripture. Everything we do should be for the glory of God. And nowhere in the Bible does it say we must deny all earthly pleasure—many are wholesome and heavenly. God is the One who pours out blessings beyond measure, and He wants us to enjoy them! (We must not worship our blessings, but rather thank God who blesses us.) *Joy* is a biblical emotion. The word *joy* appears in the NIV 218 times.

20. Let's read a small sampling of Scriptures based on *the joy of the Lord* that is available to us every day. Make note of the encouragements you come across and how they personally inspire you.

    • **Psalm 16:11**

    • **Nehemiah 8:10**

    • **Isaiah 55:12**

    • **1 Chronicles 16:26-28**

21. Does your relationship with Jesus bring you joy? Do you feel the need to be somber in order to prove your devotion to God? Or are you giving God the glory by joyfully appreciating your blessings and living in their fullness today? Elaborate.

"He put a new song in my mouth, a hymn of praise to our God." Psalm 40:3

"Rejoice always, pray continually, give thanks in all circumstances; for this is God's will for you in Christ Jesus." 1 Thessalonians 5:16-18

The best way of *refocusing our minds onto things above* and *setting our hearts on things where Christ dwells* is obviously by reading our Bibles and praying to the Lord. But there are two additional, yet essential ways of redirecting the course of our thoughts, emotions, and days: rejoicing in the Lord and counting our blessings are surefire ways of lifting our spirits. We can be having what seems like the worst day, but if we stop in our tracks and begin meditating on all the good that God has brought and continues to bring into our lives, everything instantly changes. Our perspective lifts from our surroundings and circumstances onto the goodness and grace of God. We can't help but be overcome with gratitude. We then see the world, our situations, and ourselves in a brand-new light!

"Why, my soul, are you downcast? Why so disturbed within me? Put your hope in God, for I will yet praise him, my Savior and my God." Psalm 42:5

22. Now is an excellent time to ask the Lord to call to mind all the blessings He has poured into your life; His provisions every day, past and present, and the hope He brings to your future. Thanking the Lord is the best cure for discouragement and discontentment. Count your blessings here (use a journal if you need more room):

"Blessings crown the head of the righteous..." Proverbs 10:6

One more amazing benefit to give thanks for: Paul reminds us that we have been set free from manmade commands, rituals, and misleading teachings. We follow Jesus, we belong to Him alone, and we abide solely by the Holy Scriptures. We don't have to belong to a certain church or pledge our allegiance to a specific denomination—that's a human division. We belong to the worldwide, eternal Church which is founded on the finished work and sacrifice of Jesus Christ. He is the One who qualifies us, deems us righteous, and says we are welcome to His table. Our pledge is to Jesus and only Jesus. A local church that aligns with these irrefutable truths and faithfully teaches the Scriptures is one where we can confidently worship. Let's embrace that freedom!

23. Let's take a deeper look at the freedom we have in Jesus. Read the following verses and then write them out word for word, allowing them to get firmly fixed in your mind. Then record your thoughts on what they personally mean to you.

- **Galatians 5:1**

- **2 Corinthians 3:17**

- **James 1:25**

24. *You died with Christ to the elemental spiritual forces of this world* and have been given freedom in Christ. Sin no longer has a hold on you, and death is no longer a threat. How does, or will, this freedom impact you?

Our freedom in Christ is not a liberty to sin. On the opposite end of the spectrum to asceticism, we have people who abuse the mercy, grace, and gifts of God. They continue to indulge in things that are sinful, rebellious, and harmful; and take for granted the forgiveness they have been shown. They forget all that Jesus went through to cover the debt of our sin. It is truly inexcusable!

25. Read the following verses for more on not abusing our freedom in Christ.

- **Romans 6:1-5**

- **1 Corinthians 10:23-11:1**

- **Hebrews 10:26-29**

26. How does your newfound freedom in Christ increase your desire to please Him?

"As for other matters, brothers and sisters, we instructed you how to live in order to please God, as in fact you are living. Now we ask you and urge you in the Lord Jesus to do this more and more." 1 Thessalonians 4:1

It is so much better to please the Lord, than to grieve Him!

"Therefore each of you must put off falsehood and speak truthfully to your neighbor, for we are all members of one body. [26] "In your anger do not sin": Do not let the sun go down while you are still angry, [27] and do not give the devil a foothold. [28] Anyone who has been stealing must steal no longer, but must work, doing something useful with their own hands, that they may have something to share with those in need.

[29] Do not let any unwholesome talk come out of your mouths, but only what is helpful for building others up according to their needs, that it may benefit those who listen. [30] And <u>do not grieve the Holy Spirit of God, with whom you were sealed for the day of redemption</u>. [31] Get rid of all bitterness, rage and anger, brawling and slander, along with every form of malice. [32] Be kind and compassionate to one another, forgiving each other, just as in Christ God forgave you." Ephesians 4:25-32

27. Why would the behaviors described in Ephesians *grieve* the Holy Spirit? How are they an affront to the work He desires to accomplish within us?

A few of the <u>antonyms</u> for *grieve* are *approve, be happy, be glad, praise, and delight*. While our disobedience to the work of the Holy Spirit grieves Him, our complete obedience to His promptings and leadings delights Him. I sure want to gain His praise and make Him glad of me. Don't you?

28. Please read **1 Thessalonians 5:19** and record what else our behavior can do to the Spirit within us. Why do we want to avoid this?

29. According to *Biblehub.com* the Greek definition of *quench* is to extinguish, suppress, or thwart. To *quench* the Spirit is to put out His Holy flame within us. How can we fan His flame within us instead?

30. The closer we walk with Jesus, the more we desire His ways. How is the Holy Spirit growing a hunger and thirst for righteousness in you?

The grace of God upon us should elicit great freedom, gratitude, and a surrendered life!

31. Are you setting your mind on the heavenly truths regarding your God-given identity? Describe the mental and spiritual freedom this brings.

32. As we come near the end of our lesson, do you find that you are resting in Jesus' sacrifice to make you perfect? Are you experiencing more of the joy He came to give? Please share details.

We are not bound to legalism to secure our salvation; we need not chase after mystical experiences to solidify our faith; and there is no higher knowledge that we need to seek. Our relationship with Jesus is enough to make us right with God and completely fill us up. A knowledge of Him is all that's required!

"I will walk about in freedom, for I have sought out your precepts." Psalm 119:45

An abundant life is the result of intentionally meditating on God's Word and rooting our lives in what it says. A life founded on the Bible is not easily shaken by the uncertainties of the world or swayed by the passing philosophies of culture. A truly prosperous life is one filled with the love, hope, and peace of Jesus. It is a life rooted in faith, overflowing with the joy of the Lord. It is a life that remains vibrantly alive during dry seasons, and even flourishes during times of drought. It draws refreshment from a relationship with the Savior and places its confidence in the Promises of God. It believes that God is who He says He is and that we are who He says we are. A triumphant and thriving life walks closely with the Lord. Our fullness is found in Christ!

"Oh, the joys of those who do not follow the advice of the wicked, or stand around

with sinners, or join in with mockers. But they delight in the law of the Lord,

meditating on it day and night. They are like trees planted along the riverbank,

bearing fruit each season. Their leaves never wither, and they prosper in all they do."

Psalm 1:1-3, NLT

Are you currently feeling dry and weary? Find *delight in the Law of the Lord, meditate on it day and night*, and you will feel vibrantly alive.

Look to Jesus and allow Him to revive you.

Push away the worries of the world and the pressures of daily life by leaning into the Lord's arms today. Grow your roots down deep into the Word of God and find the refreshment your soul needs.

Party Clothes

If Jesus came to give us abundant life, why are there still days when we walk around feeling numbly dead on the inside, appearing to be in mourning on the outside? I believe it is because we are forgetful of the fact that we have been set free from the curse of sin, and that we have been called out of the grave into new life and freedom. Considering our newness of life, we should be filled with hope, tearing off our old grave clothes, replacing them with *a garment of praise* (Isaiah 61:3). Reflecting on what the Lord has done for us should change our somber outlook into a countenance of grateful celebration. The unpleasant stench of death should no longer surround us, rather the sweet aroma of joy should be our new fragrance. We once were dead in our sins, but now we have been made alive in Christ. Jesus has rolled the stone away and has called us out of the dark; I think it is time we put on our party clothes and dress the part!

John 11:43-44, "When he had said this, Jesus called in a loud voice, 'Lazarus, come out!' The dead man came out, his hands and feet wrapped with strips of linen, and a cloth around his face. Jesus said to them, 'Take off the grave clothes and let him go.'"

Have you taken off your grave clothes and put on your new life in Christ? Are you living in the reality of your liberation?

—Excerpt from *"Worship and Wonder: Faith-Filled Devotions"*

Newness

There is newness of life available to us in Jesus—if only we would grab hold of and purposefully walk in this promise. We must put off the constraints of our old self and run with abandon in light of our newfound freedom. We have been set free from sin and death and the things of this world, and now live with the hope of God's Kingdom in mind. When we live in the reality of our identity in Christ, some amazing things begin to happen—joy replaces sorrow; righteousness replaces sin; forgiveness replaces condemnation; confidence replaces shame; hope replaces despair; peace replaces worries; love replaces fear. We must strip off everything that used to define and confine us and choose to walk in the new and full life to which Christ has called us. We should rejoice in our salvation and give thanks for our new position. In response to all that Jesus has done, let's count our blessings daily and praise the Lord's holy Name. Let's give glory to God by embracing and joyfully walking in the gift of new life! Let's not waste this beautiful opportunity but take advantage of our every blessing!

"We were therefore buried with him through baptism into death in order that, just as Christ was raised from the dead through the glory of the Father, we too may live a new life." Romans 6:4

What do you need to replace today? Ask the Lord to help you make the glorious exchange.

"I rise before dawn and cry for help;

I have put my hope in your word.

My eyes stay open through the watches of the night,

that I may meditate on your promises.

Hear my voice in accordance with your love;

preserve my life, LORD, according to your laws."

Psalm 119:147-149

Clothed in Christ

Colossians 3:1-4:1

How much thought did you put into your attire today? Did you know that there is more to our appearance than the clothes in our closet? Well, there absolutely is! We are about to add some essential items to our daily wardrobe.

So far in our study of Colossians, we have established the supremacy of Christ in all things, and we have affirmed our identity in Christ as beloved children of God. Today's lesson will focus on how these two foundational truths should impact and be evidenced in our lives moving forward. We are going to get clothed in Christ!

I'm sure you've noticed that our thoughts often follow a pattern. The more we think negatively, as if the sky were falling, the gloomier we will obviously feel. The more we focus on the glass half full, the more our joy will naturally overflow. What we think about, meditate on, and ruminate in greatly affects our lives. We do not have to stay stuck in our thought pattern ruts, we have the power to change our thought life by redirecting our hearts and minds onto Jesus and the hope that He brings. We don't have to keep listening to the broken record playing in our heads; we can pick up the needle and play a new song. We have Jesus as our Savior. We have the Holy Spirit living inside us. We have been cleansed of our sins and we've been made new in Christ. We are sealed with God's love and have the hope of residing in His Kingdom forever. We have a LOT to be thankful for! Our lives should be overflowing with thanks and bursting forth with praise. We should be clothed in extraordinary faith, hope, peace, joy, and gratitude.

1. How would you describe your present state of mind? What is the condition of your heart currently? Are the truths about God and yourself beginning to reframe your thought patterns? Elaborate.

2. Please read **Colossians 3:1-4:1** and record your overall observations.

We will now break our section of Scripture into smaller portions. The first verse we come upon is the theme for our entire study. We will continue taking our thoughts captive and making them obedient to Christ. We will set our hearts, we will fix our minds, we will lift our eyes, and we will live for Christ! Enjoy this lesson!

Set Your Mind on Things Above

Colossians 3:1-4, *"Since then, you have been raised with Christ, set your hearts on things above, where Christ is, seated at the right hand of God. ² Set your minds on things above, not on earthly things. ³ For you died, and your life is now hidden with Christ in God. ⁴ When Christ, who is your life, appears, then you also will appear with him in glory."*

Our identity is defined by our Creator and it is discovered through our relationship with Jesus. We live on this temporal globe, but we are citizens in the eternal Kingdom of Heaven. The things of this earth will pass away, but our place with the Father will last forever. With this in mind, we must hold loosely to this world and cling tightly to the Savior. Our hope, peace, joy, strength, and security are found in Him. The Lord has promised to return for us someday and usher us into our new Heavenly dwelling where His glory will brilliantly shine and light up the city as bright as day. **Revelation 21:23** says, *"The city does not need the sun or the moon to shine on it, for the glory of God gives it light, and the Lamb is its lamp."* Being with Jesus in Heaven is the eternal treasure that awaits us. This is our glorious future! This hope should guide and define our mindset here and now.

"For where your treasure is, there your heart will be also." Matthew 6:21

3. Are you placing your faith in the things you see around you? Or are you finding your hope in the promises of God? (Hebrews 11:1) Which would you say most often characterizes and occupies your thoughts? Explain.

4. How does the promise of Jesus' return help you to endure and persevere?

5. Let's allow the treasure of Heaven to encourage our hearts daily. Please read **Matthew 6:33-34** and record what Jesus says we should seek. How does Jesus say this will help us?

Above all else, we are commanded to seek Jesus and His Kingdom first—to set our hearts and minds on things above, where Jesus is seated in ultimate authority—and trust Him to provide for everything that follows. In this way we conquer our worries.

"How long must I wrestle with my thoughts and day after day have sorrow in my heart? How long will my enemy triumph over me?" Psalm 13:2

6. Do you wrestle with your thoughts occasionally, or on a regular basis? It's exhausting, isn't it? How do you usually overcome these battles?

Our greatest enemy is the devil himself. He is thrilled when we lose sight of how great our God is and who we are in Christ. He is overjoyed when we wrestle with doubts and are overcome with anxiety and depression. He loves when instead of setting our minds above, we let our focus sink to our ground-level surroundings. It is his hobby to steal our hope and make us feel discouraged. But Satan can only triumph over us so long as we let him.

7. Do you realize that you have a choice as to whether you allow Satan to have access and free reign in your mind? Are you ready to take back control of your thoughts? Explain.

8. Please open your Bible to the following verses and record the keys to being an overcomer in Christ.

   - **2 Corinthians 10:4-5**

   - **Philippians 4:8**

   - **2 Thessalonians 2:14-15**

9. According to **1 Peter 5:4,** what further blessing awaits us as a reward for our perseverance?

Renewed in the Knowledge

Keeping *our heart and mind set on things above* will not only change our perspective and improve our outlook, but it will also affect our attitude, behavior, words, and actions. In Christ, we have newness of life in every aspect! Paul shares some strong exhortations on how our lives must reflect the fresh start we have been given in Christ. Being that we are renewed in the knowledge of who God is and who we are in relation to Him, we must shed our old sinful self and put on the virtues of God. We are not held to the Law to earn our salvation, but we are called to a holy way of living as a means of thanksgiving for all the Lord has done.

"Thanks be to God for His indescribable gift." 2 Corinthians 9:15

Colossians 3:5-14, *"Put to death, therefore, whatever belongs to your earthly nature: sexual immorality, impurity, lust, evil desires and greed, which is idolatry. ⁶ Because of these, the wrath of God is coming. ⁷ You used to walk in these ways, in the life you once lived. ⁸ But now you must also rid yourselves of all such things as these: anger, rage, malice, slander, and filthy language from your lips. ⁹ Do not lie to each other, since you have taken off your old self with its practices ¹⁰ and have put on the new self, which is being renewed in knowledge in the image of its Creator. ¹¹ Here there is no Gentile or Jew, circumcised or uncircumcised, barbarian, Scythian, slave or free, but Christ is all, and is in all. ¹² Therefore, as God's chosen people, holy and dearly loved, clothe yourselves with compassion, kindness, humility, gentleness, and patience. ¹³ Bear with each other and forgive one another if any of you has a grievance against someone. Forgive as the Lord forgave you. ¹⁴ And over all these virtues put on love, which binds them all together in perfect unity."*

Would we rather have immorality, impurity, lust, evil desires, greed, idolatry, anger, rage, malice, slander, and filthy language define our character? Or do we desire to be known by our holiness, compassion, kindness, humility, gentleness, patience, mercy, grace, and love? The descriptions that represent the Lord's righteousness are exceedingly more appealing!

10. Please reread verses **3:11-14** and write out the virtues that we as *God's chosen people, holy and dearly loved*, must clothe ourselves in and the actions we must take:

11. The original Greek meaning of the word *bear* in this verse, means *to patiently persist*. Is there someone in your life that you need to *bear with* in the Name of Jesus? Ask the Holy Spirit to help you do so in love. You can express your prayer here if you like:

12. To what extent are we called to forgive someone? To what extent has Jesus forgiven you? How does this alter your perspective or convict you?

13. How does *love bind all these virtues together*? How have you seen this to be true in your own life and relationships?

When we are getting dressed in the morning let's also pray for the Holy Spirit to clothe us in the attitudes of Jesus and to cloak us in love. What a beautiful and striking outfit this would be!

Ever-Increasing

There is a huge disparity between our earthly nature and the Spirit of God at work in us. The comparison of the two is startlingly eye-opening. Being made new in Christ should give us a growing distaste for the behaviors and actions of the flesh and an ever-increasing hunger and thirst for the good and pure things of Christ.

14. Please read the following verses and make note of what they say in relation to this passage of Colossians. How does Scripture describe us? How should we walk and live? Who must we keep in step with? What is the overflowing fruit we will produce?

- **Romans 6:6**

- **2 Corinthians 5:17**

- **Galatians 5:16-25**

"Since we live by the Spirit, let us keep in step with the Spirit." Galatians 5:25

15. Compare and contrast your own desires and the work of the Holy Spirit within you. Does spending time in the Word and in prayer help to bridge the gap and align your will with God's more easily? Please explain.

Smack dab in the middle of this portion of Scripture, Paul explains that *in Christ* there is no distinction between *Gentile and Jew*, or any other backgrounds, ethnicities, cultures, or rankings that normally define and divide us. Paul named people who appear close to God and those who are considered the worst sinners of all, to explain that no matter who we are, we must put aside our fleshly nature and clothe ourselves in Christ. It doesn't matter if we grew up in the church or grew up on the streets—Jesus demands and creates new life in each of us!

In Christ we are all the same as we stand before God—there is no hierarchy. No matter our upbringing or our sins, we have all left our past behind us and have put on the righteousness of Christ. We are all sinners who are saved by the same Savior. We belong to the same family, and we worship the same God. We are filled with the same Holy Spirit, and we love the same Lord. We have been given the same purpose of living for the Kingdom, and we share the same hope and promise of Heaven. Paul is reminding the Colossians, and us, that everything that sought to divide and separate us before we came to faith, is canceled in the name of Jesus. Whatever baggage we brought to the table has been taken care of at the Cross by the Lord. And we need leave it there—it will only hinder us and get in the way of our relationships with others. In Jesus there is unity.

We must keep in mind that Jesus gave up His life for us, and we must die to sin and selfishness in response. When we encounter others, we must represent Jesus well and behave in a way that honors Him—putting off our sinful, prideful inclinations, putting on the heart of Jesus. We must clothe ourselves in the love and righteousness of our Savior, and approach others with the same mercy and grace with which the Father has shown us. <u>Our relationship with others is where our Christian walk will be put to the test</u>! We must remember to be fully clothed in Christ every day! *Humility* is the foundational garment in the life of a Christian. And *love* is the overcoat to all the characteristics we must put on every day.

16. For more on this topic read the following verses and record what you find.

- **Ephesians 2:11-18**

- **2 Timothy 2:22-24**

17. How does adorning yourself in the clothing of Christ help in your interactions with others? How are your perspective, demeanor, and attitude changing? Are your words and tone being affected?

As we stand before God, we are wrapped in the love and righteousness of Christ. Our identity is found in Him. In order to experience the fullness of our identity and live out the righteousness He calls us to, we must continually abide in Christ— being rooted and established in Him. We cannot be transformed in our own strength or by our own resolve.

"You are already clean because of the word I have spoken to you. [4] Remain in me, as I also remain in you. No branch can bear fruit by itself; it must remain in the vine. Neither can you bear fruit unless you remain in me. [5] "I am the vine; you are the branches. If you remain in me and I in you, you will bear much fruit; apart from me you can do nothing." John 15:3-5

18. Is abiding/remaining in Christ a priority for you? What does that look like for you? In the matter of being fruitful, do you notice the difference between striving in your own effort and leaning into the Lord? Explain.

All In the Name of Jesus

Colossians 3:15-17, *"Let the peace of Christ rule in your hearts, since as members of one body you were called to peace. And be thankful. ¹⁶ Let the message of Christ dwell among you richly as you teach and admonish one another with all wisdom through psalms, hymns, and songs from the Spirit, singing to God with gratitude in your hearts. ¹⁷ And whatever you do, whether in word or deed, do it all in the name of the Lord Jesus, giving thanks to God the Father through him."*

These verses from **Colossians 3:15-17** are especially encouraging and uplifting to our hearts. But they are more than beautiful light-hearted words, they are essential practices and mindsets that equip us to live out the instructions that follow. We must allow the peace of Christ to rule our hearts, no matter our circumstances. We must count our blessings and remember the Lord's generous provision—He saved us, redeemed us, set us free, and is with us every single day. We must let the message of Christ dwell in our hearts and give us strength to face whatever comes our way. All these *musts* are not obligations, but rather amazing opportunities for God to fill us up to the point of overflowing. Situations can be challenging, and people can be difficult, but as long as we keep our minds on things above, we will be able to respond like Jesus. He is our help for every circumstance and relationship. Whatever we do, whatever and whoever we face, we should keep in mind the sacrifice Jesus made on our behalf and live for Him in return. Paul gives us the encouragement to *let the word of Christ dwell in us richly* and to do everything in the Name of Jesus—this is in preparation for his calls to action regarding our relationships with one another, which you will find in our upcoming portion of Colossians.

19. What is the condition of your heart? Is it filled with God's peace? Is it bursting with thanksgiving, all year long? Do songs of praise and joy fill your mind and spring from your mouth? Are you filled up with the goodness of God so you can pour out to others? Please thoughtfully consider these questions and then elaborate.

20. Abiding in Jesus, dwelling in His Presence, drawing strength from His Source causes an abundant overflow to spring from our lives. Please read the verses below and make note of the specific affect and overflow.

- **Psalm 4:8**

- **Psalm 23:4-6**

- **Psalm 119:171**

- **Romans 15:13**

- **Ephesians 5:18-20**

- **Galatians 5:22**

"Therefore, since we are receiving a kingdom that cannot be shaken, let us be thankful, and so worship God acceptably with reverence and awe, [29] for our "God is a consuming fire." Hebrews 12:28-29

21. Love, joy, peace, patience, kindness, goodness, faithfulness, hope, praise, thanksgiving—what aspect of overflow do you need more of right now? Ask Jesus.

As Working for the Lord

Our preceding section from Colossians closed with the words, *"And whatever you do, whether in word or deed, do it all in the name of the Lord Jesus, giving thanks to God the Father through him."*

Paul goes on in his letter to demonstrate how we can practically implement this idea in a few of our most cherished relationships. Knowing that the people closest to us will often shake us, rub us the wrong way, and test our new mind and behavior the most, he reminds us to carefully use our words and actions towards others as if we were doing it for the Lord. This is how we show thanks to God the Father for all He has done. Talk about convicting and humbling!

Some of the following examples may resonate with you, others may not apply. Regardless, we all have close relationships of some sort and the Christ-like behaviors that Paul is calling us to live out pertain to every one of us. Mutual humility, love, and respect must be enacted in all these relationships for them to be at their best as God designed. Even if the other person in the relationship doesn't behave the way God commands, we are still accountable for our behavior towards them.

Colossians 3:18-4:1, *"Wives, submit yourselves to your husbands, as is fitting in the Lord. ¹⁹ Husbands, love your wives and do not be harsh with them. ²⁰ Children, obey your parents in everything, for this pleases the Lord. ²¹Fathers, do not embitter your children, or they will become discouraged. ²² Slaves, obey your earthly masters in everything; and do it, not only when their eye is on you and to curry their favor, but with sincerity of heart and reverence for the Lord. ²³ Whatever you do, work at it with all your heart, as working for the Lord, not for human masters, ²⁴ since you know that you will receive an inheritance from the Lord as a reward. It is the Lord Christ you are serving. ²⁵ Anyone who does wrong will be repaid for their wrongs, and there is no favoritism. ⁴:¹Masters,* *provide your slaves with what is right and fair, because you know that you also have a Master in heaven."*

The relationships between husband and wife, and parent and child are some of the closest bonds we will ever experience, but without the love of God holding them together they can also become some of our most strained.

22. How can being clothed in Christ daily impact these relationships for the better? Why is humility an essential attitude? How have you seen this in your own life?

It is impossible to clothe ourselves in the mind, character, words, and behavior of Christ by sheer willpower; we can only clothe ourselves in the likeness of Jesus by getting acquainted with Him through studying our Bibles and by coming to Him often in prayer. It is essential that we spend time in the Presence of our Lord and Savior, getting to know His heart more and more. We must also ask for the Holy Spirit to take over our hearts and lead the course of our lives—choice by choice, word by word, tone by tone, moment by moment. If we want our marriages, children, and all other relationships to reach their fullest potential and be all that God intends for them to be, He must be invited to participate. Prayer is the doorway for God to powerfully move in all our relationships.

Prayer changes everything! This is a fact!

Ideally husbands and wives would pray *together* for the sake of their marriage, but I know this is not always the case. If you and your spouse are already prayer partners, great! If your spouse is a believer and prayer is not a part of your routine, I encourage you to take some baby steps and incorporate times of prayer together—even beginning by simply saying grace before dinner, and then move on from there. If your spouse has not yet placed their faith in Jesus, do not despair—your prayers have more power than you can imagine—you can still pray for God to unite you two in amazing ways. We shouldn't approach prayer by asking God to completely change our wife or husband; we should come with humble hearts, petitioning for the Lord to unite us as one: with love, respect, kindness, goodness, and faithfulness as our clothing. We should also ask Him to search our own hearts and ask Him to reveal any hard-heartedness we harbor that needs to change. Then we can ask for God to work in our spouse's life with the purpose of bringing out the very best in them. (Check out Matthew 7:2-4.)

23. Let's put this invaluable practice into action right now. Take a moment to pray for <u>your spouse and your marriage</u>. **Genesis 2:24** tells us, *"That is why a man leaves his father and mother and is united to his wife, and they become one flesh."* Pray for the *oneness* of your marriage regularly. If you are not married, you can begin praying for the person God may want to bring into your life in the future. Know that <u>being single</u> is truly wonderful and you can pray about too—**1 Corinthians 7:32-35**. And if <u>divorce</u> is a part of your story, ask the Lord to mend and fill your heart completely. If you are <u>widowed</u>, remember that you have the promise of Heaven!

You can begin your prayer here:

"May the Lord make your love increase and overflow for each other and for

everyone else, just as ours does for you." 1 Thessalonians 3:12

I realize that the topic of marriage merits a complete study of its own. We will merely touch on the subject here. This lesson doesn't address abuse, but I encourage you to reach out to someone trustworthy and get help if you need it.

Marriage: Paul elaborates further on the topic of husbands and wives in his letter to the Ephesian church:

Ephesians 5:21-33, *"Submit to one another out of reverence for Christ. [22] Wives, submit yourselves to your own husbands as you do to the Lord. [23] For the husband is the head of the wife as Christ is the head of the church, his body, of which he is the Savior. [24] Now as the church submits to Christ, so also wives should submit to their husbands in everything. [25] Husbands, love your wives, just as Christ loved the church and gave himself up for her [26] to make her holy, cleansing her by the washing with water through the word, [27] and to present her to himself as a radiant church, without stain or wrinkle or any other blemish, but holy and blameless. [28] In this same way, husbands ought to love their wives as their own bodies. He who loves his wife loves himself. [29] After all, no one ever hated their own body, but they feed and care for their body, just as Christ does the church— [30] for we are members of his body. [31] "For this reason a man will leave his father and mother and be united to his wife, and the two will become one flesh." [32] This is a profound mystery—but I am talking about Christ and the church. [33] However, each one of you also must love his wife as he loves himself, and the wife must respect her husband."*

24. What do you learn about submission? Reverence? Love? Becoming one?

25. What are the commands to wives? For husbands?

26. What do you learn about the relation between husbands and wives and Christ and the Church? How does this impact your view of marriage?

Our marriages are intended to give an earthly glimpse of our heavenly relationship with Jesus. Jesus is our Bridegroom, and the Church is His Bride.

"Let us rejoice and be glad and give him glory!

For the wedding of the Lamb has come, and his bride has made herself ready.

[8] Fine linen, bright and clean, was given her to wear." Revelation 19:7-8

Christ submitted His life for our sake—that is true love and humility! This should stop us in our tracks the next time we have a disagreement and are tempted to stomp our foot and demand we get our own way. Let's glorify Jesus in our marriages. And let's continually make ourselves ready for His imminent return!

1 Corinthians 13:8 tells us that *love never fails*. And with God's help, our love for each other will withstand both good days and bad, until death do us part.

*Jesus says, "A new command I give you: Love one another. As I have loved you, so you must love one another." **John 13:34***

This implies that we love unconditionally, sacrificially, and extravagantly whether the other person deserves it or not. We must learn to admit when we are wrong, say we are sorry, and show forgiveness instead of withholding it. Jesus showed us how to put others first by washing His disciples' feet on the night before His death. He demonstrated the true essence of love for us to emulate.

We looked at **1 Corinthians 13** in a previous lesson, but it truly applies here too:

"Love is patient, love is kind. It does not envy, it does not boast, it is not proud. [5] It does not dishonor others, it is not self-seeking, it is not easily angered, it keeps no record of wrongs. [6] Love does not delight in evil but rejoices with the truth. [7] It always protects, always trusts, always hopes, always perseveres.

[8] Love never fails." 1 Corinthians 13:4-8

This complete passage from 1 Corinthians 13 offers a description of God's perfect love for us. Just imagine how beautiful a marriage would be if both husband and wife loved in this manner. Ask God to help you love others this perfectly too.

Parenting: In both the Old and New Testaments, the Bible includes instructions regarding the relationship between parent and child. If the Lord offers to share His knowledge and wisdom, I think we should listen. He has more children than we can imagine. Whether or not you have children of your own, God wants to use you to impact the next generation for Him.

27. Please read the following verses for wisdom on parenting.

- **Deuteronomy 4:9**

  —Are you sharing the stories of God's love, grace, goodness, and faithfulness from your own experience? Explain.

- **Deuteronomy 11:18-19**

  —Are you leading by example? Is talking about Jesus a normal part of your day? Do you notice and point out God's beautiful creation on walks outside? Do you say grace at meals and prayers at bedtime? Elaborate.

- **Psalm 127:3**

  —Do you view children as a gift from God of whom you have the blessing of shepherding and taking care of? Share.

- **Proverbs 13:24**

  —Shepherds use rods to gently prod their beloved sheep away from danger and toward the right direction. They do not use them to abuse their flock. The Lord disciplines those whom He loves—not with harshness, but with loving firmness, gentleness, and understanding mixed together. Parenting is not a passive activity; children cannot raise themselves. Why is it so vital that we actively guide children toward Jesus and away from harmful influences?

- **Proverbs 22:6**

  —Why is it essential that we give children a firm foundation of faith? Parents, don't lose heart if they wander. Just pray continually and trust that God has them in the palm of His hand.

- **Ephesians 6:4**

  —Like **Colossians 3:21**, this verse has us consider: are our demands and expectations so high and off base from what God desires for our kids that they become *embittered or exasperated* in trying to reach them? Are we nurturing each child's unique God-given interests, abilities, talents, gifts, and purpose? Let's help our children discover the Lord's path for them and then nurture it. Let's help them uncover their God-designed potential and be their loving encourager, rather than a disheartening discourager. We need to let children know they are valued and loved. Let's also really listen to them.

Don't forget to have fun with your children, give hugs, and say I love you often!

As with marriage, along with clothing ourselves in Christ (patience, kindness, gentleness, etc.), our best parenting tool is prayer. It is the greatest resource we have, and the Bible is our best parenting manual. Pray for the children in your life often! Don't give up! No matter what, keep on praying!

Here is some space for you to pause, ponder, and pray for your children. If you do not have children or grandchildren of your own, use this as an opportunity to pray for nieces, nephews, any children in your life, in the church, and for the younger generation as a whole. Your influence and prayers matter greatly!

Dear Heavenly Father,

Amen.

As far as Paul's instructions to children are concerned, and yes, we are all someone's child, we must obey our parents, and our children must obey us too. According to *Biblehub.com* the Greek root for *obey* in this verse means to *attentively listen, harken to, and be responsive.* Respectfully listening to our elders holds a wisdom all its own. We could start by putting down our phones, looking up from our computers, giving our parents our full attention. Being a good citizen in the world begins with our relationships at home. This too could be a whole separate study. (I understand that not all parents *deserve* our obedience or respect, so pray for that dynamic too. God can work miracles.)

From the Ten Commandments: "Honor your father and your mother, so that you may live long in the land the LORD your God is giving you." Exodus 20:12

All One in Christ: Although Paul does not directly tackle the horrific subject of slavery, he does address it by confronting the condition of the human heart. (The slavery he is most likely referring to is one of indentured servants, rather than the forced slavery we know from America's history.) Christ is our standard of love; He is the perfect measure of mercy and grace. He gives equal value to every life no matter their social standing. He is the judge who will bring perfect justice on everyone's behalf. Paul is seeking to turn the hearts of slaves and masters towards each other by showing them their common humanity and their unity in Christ. This same turning of hearts is necessary in all our relationships and can be aptly applied to our workplace interactions. Although we may not face slavery or be someone's servant, we do have bosses and employees. There are heads of committees and helper bees, and there is a chain of command in companies and in the military. Paul is calling us to humbly love and respect each other in the Name of Jesus, no matter our role—just like he did with husbands and wives, and parents and children.

The entire book of Philemon is devoted to the subject of reconciling a runaway slave named Onesimus (he is mentioned in the next lesson) and his owner named Philemon. They have both become Christians and Paul pleads for their new faith to change their relationship to that of brothers-in-Christ—removing all prior divisions. There is no hierarchy for those who belong to Jesus.

28. How have you seen Jesus break down walls and bridge gaps between people?

29. How has the love of Jesus humbled your heart towards others?

Setting our hearts and minds on things above and clothing ourselves in the same attitude as Christ, brings glory to God and greatly impacts all our relationships!

"Set your minds on things above, not on earthly things." Colossians 3:2

As we close our time together, please pray the following prayer aloud:

Abide

Lord, help me to not depart from You or Your ways; to not wander from Your will or the path You lay out for me; to not drift from Your Presence or leave the protective shadow of Your wings. I confess that on my own I grow weak and weary; I fall and struggle to get back up; I am forgetful of Your goodness and go off in my own direction. When I attempt to do things in my own strength and effort, I find that all those endeavors are only in vain. Without Your blessing upon me and Your sovereign Hand to guide me, all my pursuits and energies are fruitless and leave me feeling empty inside. Far too often I have spoken or acted without first inquiring of You, and each of those times I have noticed that my words fall flat, and my deeds are unsatisfying. You alone anoint me and supply all my needs. Help me to constantly abide in You. May I always give pause throughout my day, to seek You first in all things. May I rest in the blessed shelter of Your protection and find inspiration in the truth of Your words. I pray to be filled with Your Holy Spirit and to have Your Holy Word stored up in me. I desire to spend time with You daily; to sit at Your feet, be overcome in adoration, to listen and hear what You would say. I ask to be filled in Your Presence to the point of overflowing, so that whatever comes out of my mouth or is done by my hands is inspired by You.

Thank you, Lord for inviting me to abide in You! Amen.

"Remain in me, as I also remain in you. No branch can bear fruit by itself; it must remain in the vine. Neither can you bear fruit unless you remain in me." John 15:4

—Excerpt from my devotional, *"Worship and Wonder"*

"Blessed is the one

who does not walk in step with the wicked

or stand in the way that sinners take

or sit in the company of mockers,

but whose delight is in the law of the LORD,

and who meditates on his law day and night.

That person is like a tree planted by streams of water,

which yields its fruit in season

and whose leaf does not wither—

whatever they do prospers."

Psalm 1:1-3

Sustained by Christ

Colossians 4:2-18

Setting our minds on things above brings encouragement to our hearts, resolve to our thoughts, direction for our lives, and purpose to our existence. Whenever we intentionally redirect our eyes onto the Lord and His infallible Word, the world and everything in it, including our personal reality, becomes viewed with a solidly rooted, larger-than-life, hope-filled perspective. The Bible is a revelation of who God is and who we are in Christ. The Bible is the truth by which everything else is measured and it is the trustworthy guide for our lives. It exposes our sinful nature and reveals our newness in Christ. As we have already learned from Paul's letter, meditating on Scripture is the key to remaining steadfast in our faith, not easily swayed by the influences of the culture that surrounds us.

So far, by setting our hearts and minds on things above, we have established who God is through the image of Jesus Christ. We have also affirmed our identity as beloved children in the Lord. We have put off our old fleshly selves and have been clothed in the same attitude as Christ. We have seen how *that clothing* enables us to reflect Jesus in all our relationships—at home, in the workplace, and in many of our other interactions.

1. How has clothing yourself in the likeness of Jesus—*with compassion, kindness, humility, gentleness, patience, and love*—been impacting your relationships? Do you feel the difference? Do others notice it too? Elaborate.

Through Paul's closing salutations, we will now look at how setting our minds on things above and clothing ourselves in the virtues of Christ not only impacts our relationships with fellow believers in the church, but also helps us endure hardships more victoriously. I think we'll find these teachings extremely useful.

Let's keep in mind that Paul wrote this letter of encouragement to the Colossians while he was confined under house arrest in Rome. His urging that they keep their hearts and minds set on things above was obviously something that he put into practice every day.

2. Please read **Colossians 4:2-18** for a refresher of Paul's final exhortations. What highlights do you notice in the closing of his letter? What final instructions does he leave with them? What is your impression of the relationship between Paul and his brothers and sisters-in-Christ?

Devoted to Prayer

In Lesson One we touched on the subject of prayer, but it such an important topic that Paul addresses it here at the end of his letter as well, and we will too.

Colossians 4:2-6, *"Devote yourselves to prayer, being watchful and thankful. ³ And pray for us, too, that God may open a door for our message, so that we may proclaim the mystery of Christ, for which I am in chains. ⁴ Pray that I may proclaim it clearly, as I should. ⁵ Be wise in the way you act toward outsiders; make the most of every opportunity. ⁶ Let your conversation be always full of grace, seasoned with salt, so that you may know how to answer everyone."*

3. What discipline does Paul exhort us to practice in the first line of this passage? (**v.4:2**) What frame of mind should we have when we pray? Why do you think he stresses the importance of this in the life of a Christian?

4. How attentive are you to the condition of your prayer life? Would you say it's improving? How can you begin carving out more time to converse with the Lord? It's a great way to both start and end your day.

The NIV version of **Colossians 4:2** uses the word *devote*. The word piqued my interest, so I looked up some various versions of this verse on *Biblegateway.com* and discovered a beautiful depth to its meaning. I'd like to share a sampling of them to expand our understanding of what Paul was encouraging us to do:

AMP: Be persistent and devoted to prayer, being alert and focused in your prayer life with an attitude of thanksgiving.

AMPC: Be earnest and unwearied and steadfast in your prayer [life], being [both] alert and intent in [your praying] with thanksgiving.

CEB: Keep on praying and guard your prayers with thanksgiving.

CJB: Keep persisting in prayer, staying alert in it and being thankful.

CEV: Never give up praying. And when you pray, keep alert and be thankful.

DARBY: Persevere in prayer, watching in it with thanksgiving...

DRA: Be instant in prayer; watching in it with thanksgiving:

ERV: Never stop praying. Be ready for anything by praying and being thankful.

EHV: Be persistent in prayer, and as you pray, be alert and thankful.

ICB: Continue praying and keep alert. And when you pray, always thank God.

ISV: Devote yourselves to prayer. Be alert and thankful when you pray.

PHILLIPS: Always maintain the habit of prayer: be both alert and thankful as you pray.

TLB: Don't be weary in prayer; keep at it; watch for God's answers and remember to be thankful when they come.

MSG: Pray diligently. Stay alert, with your eyes wide open in gratitude.

NKJV: Continue earnestly in prayer, being vigilant in it with thanksgiving...

NLV: You must keep praying. Keep watching! Be thankful always.

NLT: Devote yourselves to prayer with an alert mind and a thankful heart.

WE: Always take time to talk to God. Put your mind on what you are saying. And thank God for what he has done.

5. What additional encouragement do you gain from these versions (who knew there were so many)? Do you have a favorite, one that especially prompts you to pray more regularly and earnestly?

Paul stresses the importance of being *devoted* to prayer. The Greek meaning of *devote* is *to attend constantly; persist, persevere in, continue steadfast in.* (Biblehub.com) Let's make up our minds to be more intentionally devoted to our prayer life with the Lord—good relationships require regular communication.

Whatever our prayer habits currently are, we can always improve and draw closer to the Lord.

6. How does a healthy prayer life keep your heart and mind set on things above? Explain.

Our prayers not only redirect our hearts and minds onto the glory, power, authority, faithfulness, goodness, kindness, grace, mercy, and love of God, they are also a pleasing aroma to the Lord. Let's flood His Throne Room with the sweet fragrance of our grateful prayers!

"May my prayer be set before you like incense; may the lifting up of my hands be

like the evening sacrifice." Psalm 141:2

It was essential for Paul and his fellow believers to stay connected to the Father on a consistent basis. The persecution they faced was relentless, and prayer was their lifeline to Jesus. Paul exhorted the Colossian church to steadfastly communicate with the Lord too. And this exhortation applies to us just the same.

In **verse 4:2**, Paul stresses the importance of being *watchful and thankful* in our prayers. We'll first look at the word *watchful* and see what wisdom we find. From the various versions of this verse that we looked at, we see that *watchful* indicates *being alert, vigilant, and intentional* in our prayers.

7. Are you intentional in your prayers, or does your mind wander and flit from idea to idea? Are you cognizant of being in the Lord's magnificent and holy Presence? Explain.

8. Please read the following verses and note what insight you gain on being *alert and watchful.*

- **Matthew 26:41**

- **1 Peter 5:8**

9. How does being *watchful*—alert and vigilant—in your prayers heighten your awareness of God's Presence and prepare you against the devil's schemes? (He wants to discourage, defeat, distract, and get you off track.) How does this cognizance impact your everyday life?

Let's look at the second half of Paul's encouragement—being *thankful* in our prayers. Rather than beginning our prayers with a long laundry list of worries, fears, discouragements, needs, wants, and complaints, we should approach our Heavenly Father with words of praise and thanksgiving for who He is and all that He has done and is currently doing in our lives. Framing our prayers in this way brings glory to God and it also changes our perspective from *me, me, me*, to *Lord, Lord, Lord*, by redirecting our minds onto His faithfulness and power. It lifts our eyes from our seemingly impossible circumstances onto our hope-filled possibilities with God. Then we can confidently bring our requests to the Lord.

"Enter his gates with thanksgiving and his courts with praise; give thanks to him

and praise his name." Psalm 100:4

10. How does counting your blessings and being *thankful* aid in lifting your spirits despite circumstances? We did this in Lesson Three, but since it's so beneficial let's do it again. Recount some of your blessings and benefits. You can't help but notice an improvement in your perspective!

"Rejoice always, [17] pray continually, [18] give thanks in all circumstances; for this is God's will for you in Christ Jesus." 1 Thessalonians 5:16-18

11. According to **1 Thessalonians 5:16-18**, how consistently should we *rejoice*? How often should we *pray*? When should we *give thanks*? Are these the hallmarks of your spiritual life? Explain.

The devil plotted against Paul and the Christian men who were present with him in Rome. He also sought to stop the spread of the Gospel and destroy the church from every side and even from within. The men had to *remain vigilant against Satan's schemes* and the plans of people who hated the church too. Despite the persecution they faced, Paul reminded his brethren to *be thankful as a means of glorifying God and reviving their own spirits*. The same is true of us individually and of our present-day church.

Being a Christian is not a solitary assignment—God calls us into fellowship not only with Himself, but with each other. We need encouragement to persevere, and reminders from those who are walking alongside us. We also need the intercessory prayers of our like-minded brothers and sisters on our behalf. Paul wraps up his letter with some final encouragement to the church and a prayer request on behalf of himself.

Intercessory Prayers

12. In **Colossians 4:3-4** Paul asks the church to pray for him. What two things does he specifically request their intercession for? We can pray these for others and for our own lives as well.

"Your kingdom is an everlasting kingdom, and your dominion endures through all

generations. The LORD *is trustworthy in all he promises and faithful in all he does."*

Psalm 145:13

Amazingly, despite being in prison, Paul's concern was not for himself—his focus was on the Kingdom of God, and how he could help grow it! His concern was always on the welfare of others and for their secure salvation. He desired prayers that the Gospel would go out in power and that he would speak the Message clearly. Paul shared the Good News of Jesus with people who visited him while under house arrest, and even the men who held him prisoner. He spent his time writing letters to various churches he had helped establish with the goal of encouraging and reminding them to remain steadfast in their faith. How about that for keeping your mind set on things above?

"And pray in the Spirit on all occasions with all kinds of prayers and requests. With

this in mind, be alert and always keep on praying for all the Lord's people. [19] *Pray*

also for me, that whenever I speak, words may be given me so that I will

fearlessly make known the mystery of the gospel, [20] *for which I am an ambassador in*

chains. Pray that I may declare it fearlessly, as I should." Ephesians 6:18-20

13. Paul understood that without a personal faith in Jesus, a person is destined for an eternity apart from the goodness and glory of God in a forsaken place called Hell. Please read **John 3:16-18** and record the significance of the Gospel Message for saving a persons' soul.

14. Are you Kingdom-minded like Paul in his passion to reach the world for Jesus? Is your heart being stirred with the importance and urgency? Pray for your loved ones' hearts to be receptive to the Gospel. Pray for the courage, boldness, words, and opportunity to share Jesus with them.

Full of Grace

Colossians 4:5-6, *"Be wise in the way you act toward outsiders; make the most of every opportunity. ⁶ Let your conversation be always full of grace, seasoned with salt, so that you may know how to answer everyone."*

Paul urges us to be *wise* and to look for opportunities to share God's love and the Gospel of salvation with people who don't know Jesus. We should use our words to season, flavor, and preserve lives—explaining the reality of sin, our need for a Savior, and how Jesus gave His life to make us right with our Heavenly Father.

"Salt is good for seasoning. But if it loses its flavor, how do you make it salty again?

You must have the qualities of salt among yourselves and live in peace with each

other." Mark 9:50

15. When you share the hope of Jesus with others is it with grace, love, and understanding, or is it with a hammer? What does Paul recommend? How can you alter your approach to be more Christ-like?

16. You and I don't need to be Bible scholars to share our faith. Please read **1 Peter 3:15** and make note of what we should be prepared to share. No one can refute your personal testimony. How would you explain the hope that Jesus has brought to *your life*?

Fellow Servants

Once we accept Jesus as our Lord and Savior, we enter the ever-growing family of God. From the moment of salvation, we are never truly alone, we gain lots of brothers and sisters-in-Christ, and we acquire ministry partners all around this big round globe.

The following verses from Colossians are a beautiful example of what it looks like to put the letter of Colossians into real life action. Paul and his friends show us how to truly put off the old self and be made new in the likeness of Christ—living whole-heartedly for the Kingdom of God.

Colossians 4:7-15, *"Tychicus will tell you all the news about me. He is a dear brother, a faithful minister and fellow servant in the Lord. ⁸ I am sending him to you for the express purpose that you may know about our circumstances and that he may encourage your hearts. ⁹ He is coming with Onesimus, our faithful and dear brother, who is one of you. They will tell you everything that is happening here. ¹⁰ My fellow prisoner Aristarchus sends you his greetings, as does Mark, the cousin of Barnabas. (You have received instructions about him; if he comes to you, welcome him.) ¹¹ Jesus, who is called Justus, also sends greetings. These are the only Jews among my co-workers for the kingdom of God, and they have proved a comfort to me. ¹² Epaphras, who is one of you and a servant of Christ Jesus, sends greetings. He is always wrestling in prayer for you, that you may stand firm in all the will of God, mature and fully assured. ¹³ I vouch for him that he is working hard for you and for those at Laodicea and Hierapolis. ¹⁴ Our dear friend Luke, the doctor, and Demas send greetings. ¹⁵ Give my greetings to the brothers and sisters at Laodicea, and to Nympha and the church in her house."*

Paul and his fellow Christians faced many difficulties and endured horrible persecution for their faith. But through Paul's life story and his sentiments regarding his companions, we glean the great importance of *leaning into the Lord* and *reaching out to others*. In Paul's letter to the Colossians, we gain some valuable information regarding the love and unity experienced between these early believers—which was only possible because they kept their eyes on Jesus.

"... let us run with perseverance the race marked out for us, ² fixing our eyes on Jesus, the pioneer and perfecter of faith. For the joy set before him he endured the cross, scorning its shame, and sat down at the right hand of the throne of God. ³ Consider him who endured such opposition from sinners, so that you will not grow weary and lose heart." Hebrews 12:1-3

They rose above their circumstances by keeping their eyes fixed on the hope of Heaven. They knew that Jesus was bigger than their situation and greater than what they could see around them. The Lord was the One who helped them overcome their differences and disagreements and walk in solidarity.

Throughout this passage we hear Paul refer to his friends as *a dear brother, a faithful minister, a servant in the Lord, a fellow prisoner, co-workers for the Kingdom, and brothers and sisters.* Although Paul commends these people for their faith in Christ, there were some rocky circumstances they had to overcome to get to this place of unity and reconciliation.

These people came from different backgrounds but found commonality in Jesus. Please take a moment to read about each of these individuals.

Tychicus was a Gentile (non-Jew) who had previously accompanied Paul on his travels to Jerusalem (Acts 20:4). He now had the honor of delivering the letter to the Colossian church.

Onesimus was a runaway slave from Colossae. He had found his way to Paul in Rome and was being sent back to his owner, Philemon, as a faithful and beloved brother.

Aristarchus was a Thessalonian (Greek) who had accompanied Paul on his missionary journey.

Mark had accompanied Paul on his first missionary journey but deserted him mid-way. Obviously, amends had been made and they were *forgiving any grievances they had against each other.* (Mark is one of the Gospel writers.)

Jesus, called Justus, was quite possibly a Roman Jew who came to faith under Paul's teaching.

Epaphras was founder of the Colossian church, and his heart was for them to continue steadfastly in their faith.

Luke was Paul's constant companion, physician, and friend, who devotedly stayed with him even in prison.

Demas was loyal to the faith until the world lured him astray. (2 Timothy 4:9)

The brothers and sisters in Laodicea were Christians in a city nearby to Colossae.

Nympha was a woman who opened her home for believers to gather in worship of the Lord.

Men, women, Gentile, Jew, slave, free, prisoner, pastor, teacher, enemy, friend—
Jesus was their common bond.

17. How does Paul affectionately describe each of these individuals?

With so many varying backgrounds it was essential that they, and we, "*as God's chosen people, holy and dearly loved, clothe yourselves with compassion, kindness, humility, gentleness, and patience. Bear with each other and forgive one another if any of you has a grievance against someone. Forgive as the Lord forgave you. And over all these virtues put on love, which binds them all together in perfect unity.*" (Colossians 3:12-14)

The benefits of being in the family of God are numerous. Paul uses words such as *encourage your hearts*, *welcome*, *a comfort*, *always wrestling in prayer for you*, *and working hard for you*, to describe the actions of his fellow believers. His relationship with the Lord and with his family-in-Christ helped him endure and persevere through the challenges of this earth. He knew how valuable and essential it is to surround ourselves with people who will encourage our faith and remind us to keep our focus on Jesus.

18. The following verses speak to the beautiful *unity* we have in Christ. Please read each Scripture and record the way Jesus and His Holy Spirit bind us together as one.

- **John 17:22-23**

- **2 Corinthians 13:11**

- **Ephesians 4:3-6**

"Make every effort to live in peace with everyone and to be holy; without holiness no one will see the Lord. [15] See to it that no one falls short of the grace of God and that no bitter root grows up to cause trouble and defile many." Hebrews 12:14-15

19. The Bible has plenty to say regarding the *encouragement* that Paul speaks of in **Colossians 4:8**. Please lookup the following verses and record what you find regarding our mutual *encouragement in the Lord.*

- **Romans 1:11-12**

- **Romans 15:4-6**

- **Philippians 2:1-5**

- **1 Thessalonians 4:17-18**

- **1 Thessalonians 5:10-15**

- **Hebrews 10:23-25**

But encourage one another daily, as long as it is called "Today," so that none of you

may be hardened by sin's deceitfulness." Hebrews 3:13

20. Is there someone who shares your faith and speaks encouragement into your life? And you into theirs? Details please.

21. Do you belong to a community of Christians who will spur you on in your relationship with Jesus? Are you a part of *a Bible study group* where you can discuss the Word of God and gain insight from each other? If yes, describe how this benefits you. If no, then I encourage you to reach out and get involved.

22. Do you have a group or an individual that you *pray* with—someone you feel confident sharing your cares, concerns, and heart with, and know that they will intercede for you in prayer? Do others feel comfortable asking you to pray for them? Explain.

Friends from all different backgrounds are lovely, but there is something extra special about having friends who are also brothers and sisters-in-Christ. These relationships take things to a much deeper level, way beyond the temporary and superficial, into the eternal and profound. They are based on our common faith in Jesus and the hope we find in Him. I can honestly say that I don't know what I would do without my siblings-in-Christ. If you don't already have one, pray now and ask the Lord to help you connect with at least one faith-friend.

Remember My Chains

Colossians 4:16-18, *"After this letter has been read to you, see that it is also read in the church of the Laodiceans and that you in turn read the letter from Laodicea. [17] Tell Archippus: "See to it that you complete the ministry you have received in the Lord." [18] I, Paul, write this greeting in my own hand. Remember my chains. Grace be with you."*

Paul addressed this letter to the Colossians, but he didn't want it to stop there. He knew there was wisdom to be shared and gained for all believers through its content. It was passed on to the Laodiceans and we are still studying it two thousand years later. I don't know about you, but I am surely gaining a greater understanding from Paul's words!

We read that Paul exhorted his friend Archippus to *complete the ministry* to which God had called him. God has a calling on each of our lives too. He has placed us on this planet at this exact time in history for a reason. He has ordained the country, city, town, and street where we now reside. He has given us our own personal sphere of influence through our family, friends, neighbors, and strangers we encounter on a regular basis. No one else has the exact ministry that we have been given.

Even if all these things change throughout our lives, our calling and purpose will remain unchanged—to share the love, hope, peace, joy, and faith found in salvation through Jesus Christ. Jesus tells us to take up our cross and follow Him. He never said to lay it down at any point—but rather we are to carry it all the way Home.

23. Take a moment to reflect on the specifics of your personal calling. Describe your sphere of influence and impact. You make a difference.

In the closing of his letter, Paul endorses the contents by letting us know that he wrote it with his own hand. He reminds us that his hope-filled message was scribed while he was physically chained, but nothing could restrain the hope and joy he had in the Lord. This should be an inspiration to us all.

24. The following verses reveal more on how we are to persevere with the same mindset Paul experienced. Read them and note the solace you find.

   • **Romans 8:16-18**

   • **Romans 8:23**

   • **2 Corinthians 1:7**

   • **2 Thessalonians 1:5**

"Praise the LORD, my soul, and forget not all his benefits—" Psalm 103:2

115

"For the Spirit God gave us does not make us timid, but gives us power, love and

self-discipline." 2 Timothy 1:7

25. Paul was able to withstand many hardships by keeping his eyes on Jesus and meditating on God's promises. **(2 Corinthians 11:21-33)** Can the same be said of you? Always, sometimes, hardly ever? Please elaborate.

26. Here are some additional verses to fill your mind with promises of hope. Write them out, meditate on them, and tuck them into your heart.

- **Matthew 5:10**

- **Romans 5:3-5**

- **Romans 8:38-39**

- **James 1:12**

David was a man who intimately understood and experienced the sustaining power and grace of God. He walked in the Presence of the Lord—The Good Shepherd—as he obediently shepherded and guarded his family's flock of sheep in the hills of Bethlehem. He courageously stepped forward and fought the giant Goliath with just a sling and a stone in the Valley of Elah. He knew that the LORD Almighty was with him and that the victory was God's alone. *"David said to the Philistine, "You come against me with sword and spear and javelin, but I come against you in the name of the LORD Almighty, the God of the armies of Israel, whom you have defied...All those gathered here will know that it is not by sword or spear that the LORD saves; for the battle is the LORD's, and he will give all of you into our hands."* (1 Samuel 17:45, 47)

Years later, King Saul sought to kill David, yet he found protection under the watchful eyes of the Lord. In the barren region of Southern Israel, the Lord led David to seek refuge in a place called En Gedi. *"And David went up from there and lived in the strongholds of En Gedi."* (1 Samuel 23:29) I have been to En Gedi and have seen with my own eyes what a beautiful oasis it is. It stands in sharp contrast to the Dead Sea which is situated nearby. Amid the surrounding flat and arid terrain emerges a towering mountain with refreshing springs flowing down from on high. Tucked into the crags of the mountain are natural caves in which David would have hidden from his enemy. It was while David was hiding from Saul that he penned some of his most inspiring praise Psalms. While in the caves of En Gedi, David was sustained by focusing on the goodness of his God. He may have begun some of his Psalms by pouring out his fears and sorrows, but about midway his gaze always shifted to Heaven, and he concluded by recounting the faithfulness of his Lord. God not only sustained David with the cool springs of water flowing down from above, but He also sustained David with His Presence and by reminding him of His assured promises.

"You, God, are my God, earnestly I seek you; I thirst for you, my whole being longs for you, in a dry and parched land where there is no water. [2] I have seen you in the sanctuary and beheld your power and your glory. [3] Because your love is better than life, my lips will glorify you. [4] I will praise you as long as I live, and in your name, I will lift up my hands. [5] I will be fully satisfied as with the richest of foods; with singing lips my mouth will praise you." Psalm 63:1-5

The best cure for a downcast soul is to put our hope in God, not in ourselves, other people, our circumstances, or in our own control, but in God alone! He has the power to help us overcome anxiety and step out of depression. He is sovereign, faithful, good, and strong. It's all about perspective—when you feel down, just look up and choose to praise! You'll see that God is there to save and sustain you, just like He was for David.

God's Word is truly the refreshment that our spirits thirst for. It's the comfort our hearts desire. It is the source of nourishment our souls require. It's the truth of which we must fill our minds. It's the compass by which we must direct our lives. God's Word is an amazing blessing. It is a pure delight to those of us who have held a Bible in our hands, thumbed through its pages, poured over its words, and allowed it to soak into every ounce of our being. God's Word has the power to sustain us through every season of life. Meditating on the Word of the Lord is a necessity for anyone who wants to flourish! It reminds us of who Jesus is and of our identity in Christ, and that we are under His constant care.

27. How is God's Word sustaining you? How does praising the Lord affect your perspective?

May the Word of the Lord sustain you today, tomorrow, and the day after!

Truly Prosperous

An abundant life is the result of meditating on God's Word and rooting our lives in what it says. A life founded on the Bible is not shaken by the uncertainties of the world or swayed by the passing philosophies of culture. A truly prosperous life is one filled with the love, hope, and the peace of Jesus. It is a life rooted in faith, overflowing with the joy of the Lord. It is a life that remains vibrantly alive during dry seasons, and even flourishes during times of drought; it draws refreshment from a relationship with the Savior and places its confidence in the promises of God. A triumphant and thriving life walks closely with the Lord!

"Oh, the joys of those who do not follow the advice of the wicked, or stand around

with sinners, or join in with mockers. But they delight in the law of the Lord,

meditating on it day and night. They are like trees planted along the riverbank,

bearing fruit each season. Their leaves never wither, and they prosper in all they do."

Psalm 1:1-3, NLT

Whenever you start to feel dry and weary, remember to reach your roots down deep into the Lord. Allow His Spirit to make you vibrantly alive. Setting our hearts and minds on things above is not a one and done; it is a continuous spiritual discipline. In order to experience the abundant life that Christ came to give us, we must consciously redirect our thoughts and hearts onto Him. The more we look for His perspective, the more naturally it becomes our own. Continue meditating on God's Word which is full of His amazing promises.

What specific promises from God do you meditate on most often? What comfort and confidence do they bring you?

"Why am I discouraged?

Why is my heart so sad?

I will put my hope in God!

I will praise him again—my Savior and my God!"

Psalm 42:5-6 NLT

Meditating on Christ

Reflecting on Truth

Congratulations! I am so proud of your dedication. You have devoted the last five weeks to studying the Bible and hopefully you are already reaping the rewards! We may have arrived at the final lesson of our study, but this is not the end of our journey with Christ. We must continue to store up His words in our heart and allow them to impact our entire being—our body, mind, and spirit.

To live the full, abundant, and perseverant life that Jesus has called us to, we must set our hearts and minds on Him and His heavenly Kingdom. We must consciously and continually take our thoughts captive and make sure they align with God's truth and will for our lives. We must remember that the Lord is with us every day and fix our eyes on the glorious hope we have stored up for us in Heaven.

Fixing our hearts and minds on Christ does not passively happen; it is something that requires our deliberate action. Over the last five lessons we have studied who Christ is, who we are in Him, and how this should impact our thoughts, words, actions, and purpose. In this lesson we will meditate on what we have learned thus far and hopefully it takes root more securely and deeper than ever before. I pray that it becomes a part of who you are—a beloved son or daughter of the Almighty King!

1. How has the study of Colossians helped reframe your thoughts regarding Jesus and your identity? What are your main takeaways so far?

In the opening pages of the study, I briefly told you about the cover photo of the workbook. The mountains and hills in the background remind me that *"My help comes from the Lord, the Maker of Heaven and earth."* (Psalm 121:1-2) No matter how big my problems seem on any given day, the Lord is always bigger. He can handle everything that I bring to Him, no matter the size; nothing is too large or trivial for Him. Something I didn't mention is that just on the other side of these mountains is the Pacific Ocean. There is a path that winds between the hills and through a valley floor that I have hiked on a few occasions. It is spectacular! From the mountains to the sea, God's creation proclaims His glory. Every flower, tree, and little creature along the way speaks to His creativity. Every tiny detail declares His great attention and care. I find that being outside in nature is a perfect place for contemplating and meditating on the Lord's power, holiness, perfection, goodness, graciousness, and His supremacy.

The world has many ideas and philosophies regarding meditation. And no surprise, they differ greatly from God's.

A secular definition of meditation is described as a practice in which an individual uses a technique—such as mindfulness, or focusing the mind on a particular object, thought, or activity—to train attention and awareness in an effort to achieve a mentally clear and emotionally calm state.

All desirable goals, but often misdirected. Meditation is practiced in numerous religions and in a variety of ways, but as usual God's ways are best.

Some meditation practices ask us to focus on our breath. And yes, concentrating on our breath can calm our hearts and stop them from racing. It may cause us to pause and rest and fill us with momentary peace, but it cannot solve our problems, lift our spirits, or fill us with lasting hope, comfort, or joy. Ultimately, focusing on our breath is still focusing on ourselves unless we are mindful of the One who gives us our breath. The Bible tells us to focus on God. *"Where does our help come from? Our help comes from the Lord, Maker of Heaven and Earth!"* (Psalm 121:1-2) God tells us to take time to step out of our busyness and consciously enter His Presence. Jesus is on the Throne, and He is the one who can fully calm our hearts—with His unfailing love, peace, promises, power, and perspective. Worldly meditation asks us to clear our minds; God's Word tells us to fill it with Truth.

In fact, Scripture warns us that an empty mind is an open invitation for the devil to fill it with his lies. (Matthew 12:43-45)

These are the things that the Bible tells us to meditate on:

Psalm 48:9, "Within your temple, O God, we meditate on your unfailing love."

Psalm 77:12, "I will consider all your works and meditate on all your mighty deeds."

Psalm 119:148, "My eyes stay open through the watches of the night, that I may meditate on your promises."

Joshua 1:8, "Keep this Book of the Law always on your lips; meditate on it day and night, so that you may be careful to do everything written in it. Then you will be prosperous and successful."

These verses remind us to meditate on God's unfailing love—a love that follows us all the days of our lives and will never leave us or forsake us. Theses verses also encourage us to think about God's mighty deeds—there is nothing too big for the Lord to handle. Knowing this assures us that we can bring all our requests to Him and that He will take care of us and our problems.

We can trust that all of God's promises are true and know without a doubt that He will follow through. If He has promised to be our safe refuge, then we know that He will. Reflecting on God's mighty works throughout the Bible and in our own lives brings the confidence that He will continue to work mightily for, in, and through us today and tomorrow too. Contemplating the glorious splendor of the Lord puts everything in its proper place and gives us a more accurate perspective. Meditating on the Lord and His ways calms our spirits like nothing else can. It leads to a prosperous life—one that's filled with God's love, peace, joy, hope, and leads to perseverance. His Word sustains us in physical, emotional, and spiritual seasons of drought.

Psalm 19:14, "May these words of my mouth and this meditation of my heart be pleasing in your sight, LORD, my Rock and my Redeemer."

These are the meditations that please the Lord. They honor Him and lead to blessings for us. We can meditate on the Lord and His ways all the time and anywhere. Inside, outside, day or night. In our quiet prayer corner, or while driving in the car. Anytime we meditate on the Lord, we know that He will meet us there. We can meditate as we read our Bibles, when we come to Him in prayer, and when we just sit quietly reflecting on His goodness, listening for His Holy Spirit to speak. Our minds' meditations will begin to flow out of our mouths, be reflected in our lives, and enable us to be a blessing to others.

Let's continue taking our thoughts captive, solidifying God's Word in our minds, and persist in believing it wholeheartedly! For our final lesson we will meditate on the life-giving principles we have gathered so far.

Hope in Christ: Colossians 1:1-14

Colossians 1:4-6, *"because we have heard of your faith in Christ Jesus and of the love you have for all God's people— ⁵ the faith and love that spring from the hope stored up for you in heaven and about which you have already heard in the true message of the gospel ⁶ that has come to you. In the same way, the gospel is bearing fruit and growing throughout the whole world—just as it has been doing among you since the day you heard it and truly understood God's grace."*

    2.   According to this verse what is *the hope stored up for you*? How does this promise affect you daily? What evidence is *springing* forth from you?

"...in the hope of eternal life, which God, who does not lie, promised before the beginning of time," Titus 1:2

———————

"And hope does not disappoint, because the love of God has been poured out within our hearts through the Holy Spirit who was given to us." Romans 5:5 NASB

The *fullness* of our hope is found in Jesus Christ; His hope leaves nothing lacking or undone. He is the hope of all creation; He is the hope for our salvation; He is the hope that carries us through each and every day. He is the hope and assurance of our eternity in Heaven where we'll someday reside with our Lord God Almighty. Let's be purposeful in allowing these truths to continually fill our minds, flood our hearts, and impact our lives. We must resolutely set our hearts and minds on things above and firmly fix our eyes on Jesus. Our hope is in Christ alone!

3. Please read the following verses and underline the words and phrases that exhort us to action.

- **Proverbs 4:25-26**, "Let your eyes look straight ahead; fix your gaze directly before you. [26] Give careful thought to the paths for your feet and be steadfast in all your ways."

- **2 Corinthians 4:18**, "So we fix our eyes not on what is seen, but on what is unseen, since what is seen is temporary, but what is unseen is eternal."

- **Hebrews 10:23**, "Let us hold unswervingly to the hope we profess, for he who promised is faithful."

- **Hebrews 12:1-3**, "And let us run with perseverance the race marked out for us, [2] fixing our eyes on Jesus, the pioneer and perfecter of faith. For the joy set before him he endured the cross, scorning its shame, and sat down at the right hand of the throne of God. [3] Consider him who endured such opposition from sinners, so that you will not grow weary and lose heart."

4. How are you consistently and actively putting these into practice? Are you noticing a more optimistic outlook on everything? Do you feel more hopeful as a result? Share the particulars please.

Christ is Supreme: Colossians 1:15-2:3

Colossians 1:15, *"The Son is the image of the invisible God, the firstborn over all creation."*

    5.   How does knowing Jesus help you better understand the nature of our Almighty God?

"The fear of the LORD *is the beginning of wisdom, and knowledge of the Holy One is understanding." Proverbs 9:10*

"You are my witnesses," declares the LORD*, "and my servant whom I have chosen, so that you may know and believe me and understand that I am he. Before me no god was formed, nor will there be one after me." Isaiah 43:10*

We must continually meditate on the indisputable reality of who Christ is—we do this by reading our Bibles regularly and reframing our perspective on truths from above. We should mindfully lift our gaze to the heavens and remember that Jesus, our Lord, sovereignly spoke everything into existence with just a few powerful words. Even the perfect rhythm of the beating heart inside our chest, gives testimony to our Creator who holds our very being in His Hands. Jesus is the Word of Life, and all life begins and ends with Him. He not only set the world in motion, but He carefully keeps it spinning. He not only knit and wove us together, but He also mends our bodies, minds, and spirits, day by day.

6. Meditate on the following verses and underline or highlight every reference to the nature of God and how He works for our good.

- **Psalm 146:6-9**, "He is the Maker of heaven and earth, the sea, and everything in them— he remains faithful forever. [7] He upholds the cause of the oppressed and gives food to the hungry. The LORD sets prisoners free, [8] the LORD gives sight to the blind, the LORD lifts up those who are bowed down, the LORD loves the righteous. [9] The LORD watches over the foreigner and sustains the fatherless and the widow, but he frustrates the ways of the wicked."

- **Isaiah 42:5-8**, "This is what God the LORD says—the Creator of the heavens, who stretches them out, who spreads out the earth with all that springs from it, who gives breath to its people, and life to those who walk on it: [6] 'I, the LORD, have called you in righteousness; I will take hold of your hand. I will keep you and will make you to be a covenant for the people and a light for the Gentiles, [7] to open eyes that are blind, to free captives from prison and to release from the dungeon those who sit in darkness. [8] I am the LORD; that is my name! I will not yield my glory to another or my praise to idols.'"

- **Psalm 27:1**, "The LORD is my light and my salvation— whom shall I fear? The LORD is the stronghold of my life— of whom shall I be afraid?"

- **Psalm 68:19-20**, "Praise be to the Lord, to God our Savior, who daily bears our burdens. [20] Our God is a God who saves; from the Sovereign LORD comes escape from death."

7. How does Christ's supremacy impact your life? What hope and comfort does the authority, power, and faithfulness of God bring?

Fullness in Christ: Colossians 2:4-23

Colossians 2:9-10, *"For in Christ all the fullness of the Deity lives in bodily form, ¹⁰ and in Christ you have been brought to fullness. He is the head over every power and authority."*

8. Are you living in the *fullness* of Christ? What does this *fullness* mean to you?

"But God demonstrates his own love for us in this: While we were still sinners, Christ died for us. ⁹ Since we have now been justified by his blood, how much more shall we be saved from God's wrath through him! ¹⁰ For if, while we were God's enemies, we were reconciled to him through the death of his Son, how much more, having been reconciled, shall we be saved through his life! ¹¹ Not only is this so, but we also boast in God through our Lord Jesus Christ, through whom we have now received reconciliation." Romans 5:8-11

———————

"Therefore, there is now no condemnation for those who are in Christ Jesus."

Romans 8:1

The fullness of God is found in Christ, and through our faith in Jesus' sacrifice we are brought to fullness too. In Jesus we find our purpose for living, we gain strength for enduring, we encounter love in its fullest expression, we are freed from condemnation, we are enabled to overcome sin and walk in righteousness. In Christ we are redeemed, justified, forgiven, reconciled, saved, adopted, chosen, included, and marked with the seal of the Holy Spirit. Through Christ we discover grace, mercy, peace, joy. In Jesus we have the hope of Heaven! Not a single detail is overlooked or missing!

9. Please underline or highlight the descriptive words and phrases regarding all Jesus has done for you and who He has made you to be.

- **Ephesians 1:1-23**, "Paul, an apostle of Christ Jesus by the will of God, To God's holy people in Ephesus, the faithful in Christ Jesus: [2] Grace and peace to you from God our Father and the Lord Jesus Christ. [3] Praise be to the God and Father of our Lord Jesus Christ, who has blessed us in the heavenly realms with every spiritual blessing in Christ. [4] For he chose us in him before the creation of the world to be holy and blameless in his sight. In love [5] he predestined us for adoption to sonship through Jesus Christ, in accordance with his pleasure and will— [6] to the praise of his glorious grace, which he has freely given us in the One he loves. [7] In him we have redemption through his blood, the forgiveness of sins, in accordance with the riches of God's grace [8] that he lavished on us. With all wisdom and understanding, [9] he made known to us the mystery of his will according to his good pleasure, which he purposed in Christ, [10] to be put into effect when the times reach their fulfillment—to bring unity to all things in heaven and on earth under Christ. [11] In him we were also chosen, having been predestined according to the plan of him who works out everything in conformity with the purpose of his will, [12] in order that we, who were the first to put our hope in Christ, might be for the praise of his glory. [13] And you also were included in Christ when you heard the message of truth, the gospel of your salvation. When you believed, you were marked in him with a seal, the promised Holy Spirit, [14] who is a deposit guaranteeing our inheritance until the redemption of those who are God's possession—to the praise of his glory. [15] For this reason, ever since I heard about your faith in the Lord Jesus and your love for all God's people, [16] I have not stopped giving thanks for you, remembering you in my prayers. [17] I keep asking that the God of our Lord Jesus Christ, the glorious Father, may give you the Spirit of wisdom and revelation, so that you may know him better. [18] I pray that the eyes of your heart may be enlightened in order that you may know the hope to which he has called you, the riches of his glorious inheritance in his holy people, [19] and his incomparably great power for us who believe. That power is the same as the mighty strength [20] he exerted when he raised Christ from the dead and seated him at his right hand in the heavenly realms, [21] far above all rule and authority, power and dominion, and every name that is invoked, not only in the present age but also in the one to come. [22] And God placed all things under his feet and appointed him to be head over everything for the church, [23] which is his body, the fullness of him who fills everything in every way."

- **Ephesians 3:16-21**, "I pray that out of his glorious riches he may strengthen you with power through his Spirit in your inner being, [17] so that Christ may dwell in your hearts through faith. And I pray that you, being rooted and established in love, [18] may have power, together with all the Lord's holy people, to grasp how wide and long and high and deep is the love of Christ, [19] and to know this love that surpasses knowledge—that you may be filled to the measure of all the fullness of God. [20] Now to him who is able to do immeasurably more than all we ask or imagine, according to his power that is at work within us, [21] to him be glory in the church and in Christ Jesus throughout all generations, for ever and ever! Amen."

10. Are you confident in all that Jesus has accomplished *for* you and *in* you, and can do *through* you? Are you taking full advantage of the spiritual blessings you've been given?

Clothed in Christ: Colossians 3:1-4:1

Colossians 3:17, *"And whatever you do, whether in word or deed, do it all in the name of the Lord Jesus, giving thanks to God the Father through him."*

11. Take a moment to consider your own thoughts, words, and actions. Do they represent your gratitude for what the Lord has done?

"...you also, like living stones, are being built into a spiritual house to be a holy priesthood, offering spiritual sacrifices acceptable to God through Jesus Christ."

1 Peter 2:5

———————

"Therefore, since we have these promises, dear friends, let us purify ourselves from everything that contaminates body and spirit, perfecting holiness out of reverence for God." 2 Corinthians 7:1

Out of gratitude for all the Lord has done in our life and by the power of His Holy Spirit working in us, we put to death the sins of our flesh and live wholeheartedly for Jesus. As we go throughout our day, we should be mindful of the fact that we are called to be a holy priesthood, sanctified (set apart) to serve the Lord. Remembering that our bodies are temples where the Holy Spirit dwells will undoubtedly help guide the choices we make and affect what we want to allow into our lives. We have been given access to the Throne Room of God, and I'm sure we want to be the best we can be and bring the greatest offerings of ourselves when we come before the Lord. So, we throw off sin and everything that holds us back and allow the Lord to continually purify us. We come before Him assured and grateful, with songs of praise overflowing from our mouths. We walk this planet with the hope of Jesus welling up within us, compelling us to share our testimony of how great our God is and what He has done for us. Reflecting on all that the Lord has done for us will ultimately be echoed in our lives. *We are in the world, but not of it. We are sanctified by the Word.* (John 17:15-19)

12. Mark all the ways being clothed in Christ produces overflow in our lives.

- **Psalm 107:1-3**, "Give thanks to the LORD, for he is good; his love endures forever.[2] Let the redeemed of the LORD tell their story— those he redeemed from the hand of the foe, [3] those he gathered from the lands, from east and west, from north and south."

- **Proverbs 16:24**, NLT, "Kind words are like honey— sweet to the soul and healthy for the body."

- **Ephesians 5:19-20**, "speaking to one another with psalms, hymns, and songs from the Spirit. Sing and make music from your heart to the Lord, [20] always giving thanks to God the Father for everything, in the name of our Lord Jesus Christ."

- **Galatians 5:22**, "But the fruit of the Spirit is love, joy, peace, forbearance, kindness, goodness, faithfulness…"

13. How is being clothed in Christ impacting the way in which you overflow?

Sustained by Christ: Colossians 4:2-18

A Biblical prescription for abundant living:

Colossians 4:2, *"Devote yourselves to prayer, being watchful and thankful."*

14. Have you been following this delightful prescription for abundant living more consistently? Recount the ways this brings cheerfulness and healing to your heart and mind.

"Restore to me the joy of your salvation and grant me a willing spirit,

to sustain me." Psalm 51:12

"Surely God is my help; the Lord is the one who sustains me." Psalm 54:4

Whenever we're tempted to proudly strive in our own effort, endure in our own strength, overcome by our own power, or try to walk our journey on our own, we will undoubtedly grow weak, weary, and feel discouraged. We must purposefully and continually lean upon the Lord. We must remember that in Him we find our fullness. He never created us to live this life alone. He encourages us to cast our eyes to Heaven, to fix our eyes on Him, to set our hearts and minds on things above where Jesus is and where we will someday reside. He reminds us that worry never solved a thing, it only steals precious time from our days and nights. Jesus tells us to cast our cares on Him and He will sustain us. He reminds us to seek His Kingdom first and promises that in doing so everything else will fall into its proper place. By setting our hearts and minds on Jesus through prayer and thanksgiving, our perspective is instantly and gloriously readjusted.

15. Please highlight all the references to the ways the Lord sustains you.

- **Psalm 55:22**, "Cast your cares on the LORD and he will sustain you; he will never let the righteous be shaken."

- **Psalm 3:5**, "I lie down and sleep; I wake again, because the LORD sustains me."

- **Psalm 41:3**, "The LORD sustains them on their sickbed and restores them from their bed of illness."

- **Psalm 63:7-8**, "Because you are my help, I sing in the shadow of your wings. [8] I cling to you; your right hand upholds me."

16. Detail some of the ways God has sustained you in the past and how He is currently sustaining you.

Continue in Your Faith

Colossians 1:23, "if you <u>continue in your faith</u>, established and firm, and do not move from the hope held out in the gospel."

Colossians 1:23 NLT, "But you must <u>continue to believe this truth</u> and stand firmly in it. Don't drift away from the assurance you received when you heard the Good News."

Colossians 2:6-7, "So then, just as you received Christ Jesus as Lord, <u>continue to live your lives in him</u>, [7] rooted and built up in him, strengthened in the faith as you were taught, and overflowing with thankfulness."

Thank you for joining me on this magnificent journey! I hope that you have been blessed and inspired by our study of Colossians. God's Word is surely living and active. It has the power to transform our lives. So, let's keep reading our Bibles— the Lord has so much more to say. Your journey continues onward from here!

On the following pages you will find some short devotions to help you *continue fixing your mind on things above.* They are perfect for starting your day, while enjoying your morning coffee, or grabbing a few minutes away from the kids alone in the bathroom. You can also read a page before closing your eyes at night, so that your mind is prepped and ready for sweet dreams. I pray that you tuck all the treasures we have gathered from Scripture into your heart and allow them to bless your soul.

Love and blessings, Tracy

Easy and Light

With so many voices and things vying for our attention, pulling us this way and that with the intention of dragging us down, I do believe we need a breath of fresh air.

Amid overwhelming circumstances, anger, fear, division, personal trials, and worldly tribulations we need to refocus on *who God is* and on *our identity in Christ*. God is sovereign over everything in Heaven and on the Earth (despite what we may feel, He has everything under control). We are His beloved children who are more than conquerors through Christ who loves us. Living in the reality of these two truths will change our perspective, give us hope, fill us with joy, and flood us with His peace despite anything we face. We'll be better able to live and love like Jesus in a world that desperately needs Him.

Jesus invites *"all who are weary and burdened to come to Him, and He will give us rest."* He offers to lighten our loads and even carry them for us. We would be wise to take Him up on His gracious offer. Remember *who God is* and *who you are in relation to Him*; claim His abundant promises for yourself and confidently stand on the truth of His infallible Word. Turn your cares and concerns over to His capable hands—He's got this, and He's got you! Abide in Jesus—anchor your life securely to Him. Let Him free you of your burdens and release you from your anxious fears. Allow Jesus to fill you up and overflow through your life to everyone around! Show the world what it truly looks like to be a child of God—peace-filled, hopeful, joyous, and full of gracious love. These are the *easy and light* things that the Lord supplies to those who love and trust in Him!

Matthew 11:28-30, "Come to me, all you who are weary and burdened, and I will give you rest. Take my yoke upon you and learn from me, for I am gentle and humble in heart, and you will find rest for your souls. For my yoke is easy and my burden is light."   —Excerpt from *"Worship and Wonder: Faith-Filled Devotions"*

Hope and Confidence

Lord, You are sovereign over the day and the night, over the dark and the light, over things seen and unseen to my naked eyes. You are in complete control over everything. Thank You, Lord, that I can rest in Your omnipotent care and find refuge in Your holy Presence. Every detail of my life is laid bare before You. From before the day of my birth until the moment I step into glory, You faithfully watch over me. Thank you, God, for never leaving or forsaking me, even on my worst days and during my wayward times. There is nothing taking place on this planet of which You are not acutely aware. The world may have gone astray and seems to be in chaos, but You are good, and that never changes. You are with me throughout my circumstances, trials, tribulations, and my celebrations. My hope, peace, and joy cannot be shaken, as long as I continue to trust in You. Help me to remember that my life, and this world, are in Your fully capable Hands. You alone are my hope and confidence. Thank You, Jesus. Amen.

"For you have been my hope, Sovereign LORD, my confidence since my youth.

From birth I have relied on you; you brought me forth from my mother's womb.

I will ever praise you."

Psalm 71:5-6

How does this frame of mind impact your hope, peace, and joy?

Focus

All around us, we see evidence that our world will not last forever in its present condition. Things rust, the earth quakes, flowers fade, and hearts break. Only the promises of God and the Kingdom of Heaven will remain unchanged forever—they are our hope of eternal value. This hope we have is secure and should remain our confident focus—helping us navigate our way on this earth as we journey toward our future home in Heaven. As we walk with the Lord daily, we are constantly moving toward a future Day of perfection, when everything will be made new—someday we will be redeemed, the earth will be reclaimed by God, and the heavens will declare His glory. We will walk in the Light of God's goodness, and all evil will disappear. For now, we must focus on our heavenly hope, knowing that someday God's promises will come into focus and become perfectly clear! There are amazing blessings on the horizon for you and me!

Revelation 21:1, "Then I saw a new heaven and a new earth, for the old heaven and the old earth had disappeared."

Hebrews 11:16, "Instead, they were longing for a better country—a heavenly one. Therefore God is not ashamed to be called their God, for he has prepared a city for them."

How does focusing your eyes on Heaven help keep you from being discouraged here and now?

Draw Strength

God is the source of all our life. Everything we have emanates from Him—

Our physical life, our spiritual life, our eternal life, and our abundant life are all found in Him alone.

God fills our lungs with life-giving air on the day of our birth. He fills us with His life-changing Holy Spirit on the day of our salvation. He invites us into His Heavenly Kingdom to dwell with Him forever. He pours out endless blessings as we reside here on the earth. In Him we find our real identity—we are children of the Most High God; we are royalty. We are saved, redeemed, forgiven, and set free. In God alone, we find our purpose and reason for living. He is the source of our confidence, our hope, our peace, our joy, and our strength. If we ever find ourselves running on empty, it's because we've gone rogue and were trying to do it all alone! We must surrender our body and spirit, our future and present to His capable hands. *Just as we received Christ as Lord, we must continue in Him.* We must continue to be *rooted and built up in Him* (Colossians 2:6-7).

In the outstretched arms of our Savior, we encounter the fullest expression of sacrificial love, and an invitation to experience life in all its glory. I encourage you to lean into the Lord more and more each day and draw strength from Him with every aspect of your being.

"'For in him we live and move and have our being.' As some of your own poets have said, 'We are his offspring.'" Acts 17:28

How can you purposefully draw strength from the Lord today? In this moment?

Celebrate

"They celebrate your abundant goodness and joyfully sing of your righteousness. The LORD is gracious and compassionate, slow to anger and rich in love. The LORD is good to all; he has compassion on all he has made." Psalm 145:7-9

These Scriptures fill my mind with images of great rejoicing—the grandest celebration and feast where the Lord is the center of attention, but the guests partake in all the blessings. The Lord's House is abounding in goodness and righteousness; in His Presence, there is no bad thing. There is grace and compassion for those who enter in and partake in all He has to offer. In His heavenly House, the walls reverberate with joyful singing and praise. The sound wafts through open doors and drifts through the streets, inviting all to enter in and join the festivities. These verses bring peace to my heart and fill me with anticipation. They evoke feelings of gratitude and yield a longing to see Jesus' face. Until that glorious day, I will continue to rejoice!

What emotions do these verses evoke in you?

Reflection

How do we best reflect Jesus in this world? With gentleness, moderation, reasonableness, consideration, and a gentle spirit.

Philippians 4:5, "Let your <u>gentleness</u> be evident to all. The Lord is near." NIV

KJV—moderation

ESV—reasonableness

NASB—gentle spirit

"Let everyone see that you are <u>considerate</u> in all you do. Remember, the Lord is coming

soon." NLT

Lord, I pray that as I wait for Your glorious return, You would help me to remain steadfast in my faith, rooted in Your love, and overflowing with kindness—representing You well in everything I say and do. Help me to put others first, considering their needs above my own. Help me to live and love with You always at the forefront of my mind and remember that You are coming soon. Use me to point others to Jesus, so that they may be ready and eager for that Day too. You are good and gracious, full of mercy and kindness. May my life be a reflection of all that is true of You. Amen.

How is your life reflecting the gentleness of Jesus today?

Cookie Dough Comfort

I need Jesus every day, but occasionally I need some cookie dough too.

As a young girl I often visited my grandparents, staying over for the weekend. My Grandma and I made chocolate chip cookies on almost every one of these occasions. I would sit on her teal blue stool, and she would stand by my side, handing me the ingredients and overseeing my little hands stir. I know the recipe by heart and even though my Grandma has long since passed, I continue to make chocolate chip cookies often. There is not a day where making cookies does not fit the bill—rainy days feel cozier with the warm smell of vanilla and chocolate wafting through the air; sunny days feels even brighter with a bite of cookie dough melting on my tongue; sad days feel happy, and happy days feels even happier. I am not looking to food as my comfort per se, but to the memories that accompany the baking (and tasting) process. As I measure and scoop, and crack the egg, I pause and reflect on the past, present, and future. I remember my Grandma: the sound of her voice, the touch of her hands, and I thank God for blessing me with her and for these sweet memories I have. I think how much I miss her, and how I wish she were still here. I also grab hold of God's promises and know that I will see her beautiful face in Heaven on some glorious future day.

I always needs Jesus, but somedays I also need a spoonful of reminiscent cookie dough.

Jesus is my Rock, my Peace, my Hope, my Joy, my Salvation. He is my True Source of comfort and love. He is so good and kind though, that He puts people in His children's lives to be a source of comfort and love too.

"May your unfailing love be my comfort, according to your promise to your servant."

Psalm 119:76

Do you need Jesus and a bite of cookie dough today?

—Excerpt from my devotional, *"Worship and Wonder."*

This is a picture of Grandma Mary, Tata, and me.

Grandma and I enjoyed making the cookies, and Tata loved to eat them.

Turn the page and you'll find the recipe!

Chocolate Chip Cookie Recipe

This is the recipe that Grandma and I used:

Ingredients:

2 sticks of softened butter

¾ cup of white sugar

¾ cup of brown sugar

1 teaspoon of vanilla

2 eggs

2 ½ cups of flour

1 teaspoon of salt

1 teaspoon of baking soda

1 bag of chocolate chips

Preheat oven to 375 degrees. Mix the butter and sugar together until light and fluffy. Add vanilla and eggs and mix some more.

In a separate bowl mix the dry ingredients—flour, salt, and baking soda. Then slowly add into the wet mixture and mix until blended. Don't over-mix.

Add the chocolate chips. You're not supposed to eat the batter, but I always do.

Bake for 8-11 minutes depending on whether you like soft or crunchy cookies.

Sometimes I alter the recipe by using all brown sugar or incorporating whole wheat flour. Occasionally I add dry oats or chopped walnuts. Cut recipe in half if you like or freeze the extras to keep on hand for another day. They are great for sharing with neighbors too. Make the recipe your own and enjoy! Yum. Yum.

You Call

As I previously said, when I was a young girl, I was blessed to spend a lot of time with my grandparents. I often spent weekends at their house. If I had to pick one place on this planet that represents home, it would be under their roof. Besides baking cookies, building houses with cards, taking walks, dancing in the rain, playing games, and reading books snuggled close on the couch, I learned to stand in the front yard under the canopy of the night sky and look at the stars. I will always remember the night my Grandma took me outside to the driveway and showed me the Big and Little Dippers shining brightly against the blackness above our heads. Although many years have passed, I still search for those constellations. They recall precious memories of my Grandma, but they also remind me of the sovereignty of our God. The stars are proof of His power and goodness to us. He created every star and calls them by name, turning them on one by one to light our way even in the darkest of nights. Stars are a reminder that God does not sleep but stays awake, constantly watching over the earth and over our lives. The brilliance of stars points us to God's glory. (Ps. 19:1)

"He heals the brokenhearted and bandages their wounds. ⁴ He counts the stars and calls them all by name. ⁵ How great is our Lord! His power is absolute! His understanding is beyond comprehension!" Psalm 147:3-5

Lord, if You hold the stars in place, then You can certainly fit my heart in the palm of Your Hand. You are mighty in Your power and tender in Your love. You see the depths of my soul and have an understanding of me that I barely begin to grasp myself. You are sovereign over my past, present, and future. You have called each star out by name since the beginning of creation. You have called me by name and drawn me near through salvation. You call my name daily and invite me to walk with You. I am humbled and grateful to have fellowship with the Lord who made me. Thank you, Jesus, for continually calling my name. Amen.

Do you hear the Lord calling your name? How will you respond?

Almighty

"Who has measured the waters in the hollow of his hand, or with the breadth of his hand marked off the heavens? Who has held the dust of the earth in a basket, or weighed the mountains on the scales and the hills in a balance?" Isaiah 40:12

The Lord God Almighty has created everything in the heavens and on the earth. Everything we see with our eyes and everything beyond our limited vision fits within the palm of God's hand! His greatness exceeds what our finite minds can fully comprehend. And yet, He chooses to invite us into a personal relationship. The Lord of the universe wants us to know Him, to trust Him, to love Him, to draw near to Him, and to walk with Him daily. He offers us His strength to uphold us and His power to sustain us. He desires to be the shelter for our storms and the refuge where we find rest.

The God who spoke creation into existence with just a word wants to speak words of hope, peace, joy, purpose, and contentment to each of us.

The Lord is powerful and mighty and intimate and close!

How does the power of God and your access to His Presence comfort you today?

Push away the worries of the world and press into the Lord today. Grow deeper and thrive.

Boundless Love

God has loved you since before you were even born and He has been relentlessly drawing you to Himself—wooing and calling you into a personal relationship. He is not far off and distant, but rather loving, kind, good, and present. He desires that you don't just know about Him, but that you intimately know Him for yourself.

Deuteronomy 4:29 says, *"But if from there you seek the LORD your God, you will find him if you seek him with all your heart and with all your soul."*

God is standing with His arms open wide, ready to welcome and receive you. You need only turn and seek Him, and surely you will find Him ready to embrace you. You will find rest and refreshment for your weary soul.

Psalm 36:5 describes God's endless, immeasurable love, *"Your love, LORD, reaches to the heavens, your faithfulness to the skies."*

I encourage you to take a step outside and gaze up, casting your eyes to the heavens. I hope you notice that no matter how hard you squint or try, you'll never be able to see the furthest boundaries of the skies. They go on and on beyond our imagination—there are galaxies beyond the heavens that will never even be discovered. And just as the heavens are boundless, so is the love and faithfulness of God. No matter what your experience with love has been before, God's love surpasses it all.

Romans 8:39 reminds us that, *"Neither height nor depth, nor anything else in all creation, will be able to separate us from the love of God that is in Christ Jesus our Lord."*

There is nowhere that you can run that God's love will not follow. His love will pursue you to the ends of the earth.

What comfort does God's boundless love bring to you?

Fully Present

There are times when I feel distracted and focused on too many things at once. I feel the desire to stretch my time and fit in too much, and in the process, I miss the moment I am meant to be present in. The verses from my study time today reminded me to not toil or spin, but rest in the Lord and have faith. The Lord laid the following prayer on my heart, and I thought I would share it just in case this wrestling resonates with you.

Lord, You are sovereign over every detail of my life—every single moment, every hour, every day, and every bit of my future forever. Help me to set my life according to the rhythm and timing that You have purposed for me. Help me to live with my heart set on You and walk worthy in the fullness of Your peace. Help me to focus my mind on You and be fully present in every encounter and situation. Help me to prioritize my time according to Your schedule and trust that You will equip me to get done the things that need to get done and enable me to let go of the things that can wait. Lord, Your ways are perfect, help me to look to You as I press on toward my hope-filled Destination. Amen.

"For this reason we also, since the day we heard it, do not cease to pray for you, and to ask that you may be filled with the knowledge of His will in all wisdom and spiritual understanding; [10]that you may walk worthy of the Lord, fully pleasing Him, being fruitful in every good work and increasing in the knowledge of God..."

Colossians 1:9-10

How is the Lord calling you to be more present in the moment? With Him? With family? Friends?

Take Courage

"Immediately Jesus made the disciples get into the boat and go on ahead of him to the other side, while he dismissed the crowd. [23] After he had dismissed them, he went up on a mountainside by himself to pray. Later that night, he was there alone, [24] and the boat was already a considerable distance from land, buffeted by the waves because the wind was against it. [25] Shortly before dawn Jesus went out to them, walking on the lake. [26] When the disciples saw him walking on the lake, they were terrified. 'It's a ghost,' they said, and cried out in fear. [27] But Jesus immediately said to them: 'Take courage! It is I. Don't be afraid.'

[28] 'Lord, if it's you,' Peter replied, 'tell me to come to you on the water.' [29] 'Come,' he said.

Then Peter got down out of the boat, walked on the water and came toward Jesus. [30] But when he saw the wind, he was afraid and, beginning to sink, cried out, 'Lord, save me!' [31] Immediately Jesus reached out his hand and caught him. 'You of little faith,' he said, 'why did you doubt?' [32] And when they climbed into the boat, the wind died down." Matthew 14:22-32

This story of Peter reminds us just how vital the direction of our focus is. Peter confidently stepped out of the boat and walked toward Jesus even though the wind and waves buffeted and raged all around him. With his eyes locked onto Jesus he walked on the surface of the water. (What we are able to accomplish when we keep our eyes on Jesus is truly astounding!) Peter bravely overcame unsurmountable obstacles because he knew the Lord was near. It wasn't until he lost focus—catching sight of the tumultuous waves and noticing the forceful gale rush past his face—that he began to sink. Fear rose within him and obscured his sight of Jesus. He turned his full attention to the wind, forgetting that Jesus was with him. And we so often do the same.

Like Peter, we start off looking to the Lord as our source of comfort and strength. We draw near to Him and feel incredibly safe, even as the storms of life swirl about. Then unfortunately we begin to lose focus—a thought pops into our heads, and we have a moment of doubt that grows into overwhelming fears. Our situation seems to loom ever closer before us, and we feel the weight of everything pressing in from all around. It's in this instant that Jesus calls for our attention, reaches out, grabs hold of our hand, and catches us before we fall too far. He reminds us of His Presence and encourages us to keep our eyes firmly fixed on Him. Jesus assures us that He is with us in the storm, and not only that, but He is also in complete authority over the severest of tempests.

Whenever we feel as if we're sinking, its most likely because we have taken our eyes off Jesus. It's times like these that we must refocus, draw near, and grab hold of our Lord. He will pull us back up to a place where we can catch our breath.

What comfort do find in knowing that Jesus is with you in your storms? How can this keep you from sinking?

Worthy

Lord, help me to live a life worthy of the salvation You purchased for me. May I live in gratitude for the mercy and grace You poured out through the Cross. May I live in obedience to the calling You have placed on my life. Just as You humbly gave Your life for me and gently called my name, help me to surrender my life to You in return. And may I live humbly and gently in relation to others. Day after day, You are patient with me—my weaknesses, my sins, my waywardness, and my all-too-often forgetfulness do not push You away. Rather, You continually pursue me! In the same manner, help me to be patient with those You put in my path. You bear with me in love, even at times when I am completely unlovable. Help me to love others in the same steadfast way.

Please help me to live my life worthy of who You have made me to be. May I live in a constant state of grace and obedience—allowing your Holy Spirit to work in and through my life.

I count it pure joy to live for You and walk as You walked. Lord, please sustain me in all things.

Amen.

"As a prisoner for the Lord, then, I urge you to live a life worthy of the calling you have received. [2] Be completely humble and gentle; be patient, bearing with one another in love." Ephesians 4:1-2

Reflect on how the Lord treats you. How can you live worthy in response?

"One generation commends your works to another;

they tell of your mighty acts.

They speak of the glorious splendor of your majesty—

and I will meditate on your wonderful works.

They tell of the power of your awesome works—

and I will proclaim your great deeds."

Psalm 145:4-6

Leader Guide

Suggestions for Small Group Discussions

My short summary videos are designed to be watched after you have completed your homework for each lesson. The videos can be found on my website: https://www.beblessedandinspired.com/videos

Introduction

Here are a couple ideas to help you kick-off your study group and get you started:

1. Grab a coffee, get comfy, open in prayer, and get to know each other. (These are your sisters-in-Christ and partners for the journey.)
2. Remind everyone that this is a safe place for sharing hearts and prayer requests. Everything must be kept confidential within the group. Try to stay on topic so everyone has time to share.
3. Go around and takes turns introducing yourselves and briefly sharing a little information—name, favorite food, hobby (mine is taking long walks outside—it always clears my head), or anything else you think would be good, fun, or interesting.
4. Ask: What drew you to this study and what do you hope to gain from it?
5. Watch short *Introduction* video and close your time together in prayer. Get ready to dive into Lesson One.

Lesson One—Hope in Christ

1. Open in prayer. Share overall impressions of the lesson—greatest takeaway and encouragement.
2. Watch the summary video for *Lesson One.*
3. Have someone read **Colossians 1:1-14** aloud.
4. In our study we read about Paul and Timothy's encounters with the Lord and the radical effect He had on their lives. Making it personal: discuss questions 12, 13, and 14 with the group.
5. Discuss the Scriptures from question 19.
6. Review questions 24, 29, 36, 37, and 38. Share thoughts and comments.
7. Close your time together in prayer.

Lesson Two—Christ is Supreme

1. Open in prayer. Share overall impressions of the lesson—greatest takeaway and encouragement.
2. Watch the brief summary video for *Lesson Two*.
3. Ask a volunteer to read **Colossians 1:15-2:3** as the group follows along.
4. Turn to question 1 and discuss your answers. (Your understanding of the Lord will grow over the course of our study.)
5. Go over questions 6 and 7 and discuss the authority of God together.
6. Discuss the verses from question 9 and personalize it with question 10.
7. Discuss the way we are *reconciled* in questions 17 and 18.
8. Discuss *the supremacy of Christ* in questions 26, 27, and 28.
9. Close your time together in prayer.

Lesson Three—Fullness in Christ

1. Open in prayer. Share overall impressions of the lesson—greatest takeaway and encouragement.
2. Watch the corresponding video for *Lesson Three*.
3. Have someone read **Colossians 2:4-23** aloud.
4. As a refresher of Lesson Two, discuss questions 2 and 3.
5. Share thoughts from question 5.
6. Discuss the *practices* listed in question 8.
7. Discuss questions 20 and 21—*the joy of the Lord*.
8. Discuss *the freedom we have in Christ* by looking at questions 23 and 24.
9. Close your time together in prayer.

Lesson Four—Clothed in Christ

1. Open in prayer. Share overall impressions of the lesson—greatest takeaway and encouragement.
2. Watch the corresponding video for *Lesson Four*.
3. Ask someone from the group to read **Colossians 3:1-4:1** aloud.
4. Give the opportunity to share responses to question 1 in the workbook.
5. Discuss question 4 regarding *the hope of Jesus' return*.
6. Read Psalm 13:2 aloud and discuss question 6. Now look at question 8.
7. Discuss questions 14, 15, 17, and 18.
8. Look at the verses in question 20; then share thoughts from question 21.
9. Conclude your time together in prayer.

Lesson Five—Sustained by Christ

1. Open in prayer. Share overall impressions of the lesson—greatest takeaway and encouragement.
2. Watch the corresponding video for *Lesson Five*.
3. Have a volunteer read **Colossians 4:2-18** aloud as everyone follows along.
4. Discuss the highlights of Paul's final exhortations—question 2.
5. Look at questions 6, 7, and 9—*a healthy prayer life*.
6. Discuss the *encouragement* we gain from the verses in question 19.
7. Read the verses from question 24 and discuss how our mindset affects *our perseverance*.
8. Look at the verses in question 26 and then discuss question 27.
9. Close your time together in prayer.

Lesson Six—Meditating on Christ

1. Open in prayer. Share overall impressions of the lesson—greatest takeaway and encouragement.
2. Watch the corresponding video for *Lesson Six*.
3. Discuss question 1—*your main takeaways from Colossians*.
4. Take turns reading the Scriptures from question 3 aloud, and then answer question 4.
5. Select one of the Scriptures from question 6 to read aloud and then discuss question 7.
6. Read Ephesians 3:16-21 and then share reflections from question 10.
7. Choose a verse from question 12 to read aloud. Discuss question 13.
8. Read Psalm 54:4 and the verses from question 15. Discuss question 16.
9. Conclude your time together in prayer.

So Grateful...

For the support and encouragement from all my Bible study friends and leaders at Club 31 over the years. Thank you for teaching me to appreciate the fullness of the Word of God and helping me to see how it applies to my life.

For my family—Russell, Camden, and Christian. For continuing to support me in ministry. For helping me with my podcasts and videos and making my book cover so beautiful! Thank you for our fun times together and the love that we share. You are my greatest blessings!

For Ruthie—thank you for devoting your time to editing this book. And for being the best neighbor I could hope for. I'm glad you like cookies too.

For my dear friend Carolyn—your friendship and encouragement really bless my heart!

A Bit About Tracy...

First and foremost, I am a woman who loves the Lord with all her heart. I am married to a wonderful man, and I am a mother of two young men (who used to be little boys). I am a daughter, a sister, a friend, a neighbor. I had a beloved dog for 17 wonderful years. I enjoy taking walks outside, I like chips and salsa, I enjoy traveling, and taking pictures... and my list goes on. I love serving in the women's

ministry at my church. I enjoy leading Bible studies and teaching others about the hope, joy, peace, and confidence that is rightfully theirs as children of God. I write to inspire others to deepen their relationships with Jesus through the study of His Word. Even if our lives don't look exactly alike, I'm sure we have plenty in common. We each have ups and downs and face good days and bad. I truly thank you for joining me on this journey and hope that you find encouragement as we seek the Lord together.

Let's connect for some fellowship!

Follow my blog, listen to podcasts, see video teachings, peek at my other books, and connect with me at my website: beblessedandinspired.com

Find short and sweet devotions, and connect with me on Facebook at: facebook.com/tracyhillauthor

My podcast can also be listened to on Spotify and Anchor: Be Blessed and Inspired with Tracy Hill

Additional Inspiration...

More of my titles that are available in stores and online:

A Daughter of the King: Gaining Confidence as a Child of God (A Bible Study)—God's desire is for you to discover the confidence and rich blessings of your identity which are found in Jesus Christ. The enemy wants you to believe otherwise, so you are going to learn to fight off the lies of insecurity with Truth. You are meant to live in victory as *A Daughter of the King*. You are royalty.

Matthew: Your Kingdom Come (A Bible Study)—By studying this amazing Gospel, we will come to know Jesus better and, as a result, fall even more deeply in love with Him. We will hear His teachings, witness His miracles, see His power, feel His love. Encountering Jesus changes our lives forever.

Worship and Wonder: Faith-Filled Devotions—Throughout this devotional, you and I will meditate on God's Word and find comfort in His lavish love. We will be overcome with wonder and worship His holy Name. Every page is filled with inspiration meant to remind us of our blessings, fill us with hope, and grow our faith.

Promise and Possibilities: Hope-Filled Devotions—You will glimpse the promise that life holds and the possibility of all that can be when you place your hope in Jesus. He is truly the One who holds the key.

Confidence and Crowns: Devotions for A Daughter of the King—The devotions, stories, and Scripture you will encounter, are all intended to point you to the reality of who you are in God's eyes. It is time to put aside your doubts and insecurities and live a life of confidence.

Lilies and Lemonade: Joy-Filled Devotions—*Lilies and Lemonade* represents two philosophies which hold the key to optimistic living. A joy-filled perspective is available to us when we look at life with the proper Jesus-filled mindset.